The
French Foreign Legion

The
French Foreign
Legion

John Laffin

BARNES
&NOBLE
BOOKS
NEW YORK

This edition published by Barnes & Noble, Inc.,
by arrangement with John Laffin

1995 Barnes & Noble Books

ISBN 1-56619-806-2

Printed and bound in the United States of America

M 9 8 7 6 5 4 3 2 1

Contents

Author's Acknowledgments

My sources and bibliography will be found elsewhere. Here I must thank the French Ministry of Defence and Army Headquarters and, in particular, Captain Ribuot, for permission to inspect records and files of the Legion. Also I appreciate the recollections and opinions of serving and retired Legion officers and men, all of whom, by tradition, prefer to remain anonymous. My assistant, as always, was my wife and again I thank her for her helpful criticisms and for the immense amount of typing that goes into a completed manuscript. Mr T. J. Fallon kindly helped me with translations for the Foreign Legion songs.

For permission to quote from published material I thank the following:

Hutchinson Publishing Group (Jarrolds & Co.), publishers of *In Morocco with the Legion* by G. Ward Price; George Allen & Unwin, publishers of *Hell in the Foreign Legion* by Ernst Loehndorff; the heirs of Zinovi Pechkoff for the extract from his book, *The Bugle Sounds*; the heirs of Prince Aage of Denmark for the extract from *My Life in the Foreign Legion*; Mrs Woodall Marshall for the letter by Legionnaire Woodall Marshall quoted in Chapter 11.

It has not been possible to trace the copyright holders of *The Cohort of the Damned* by E. Duplesis, 'as told to E. C. Trelawney-Ansell'; of *Bloodspots on the Sand* by Francis A. Waterhouse 'as told to Roger L. Wimbush'; or of *The Legion of the Damned* by Bennett J. Doty. No reply was received from the publishers of Geoffrey Bocca's book, *La Légion*, or from the publishers of Charles Mercer's *The Foreign Legion*. I recommend both books for those who wish to know even more about the Legion, but they are out of print.

By far the best personal experience accounts of Legion life published in any language in the last twenty years are Colin John's *Nothing to Lose* and Henry Ainley's *In Order to Die*; the best date-and-fact history is Edgar O'Ballance's *The Foreign Legion*. Again, these books are long out of print.

'Non, je ne regrette rien'
(No, I regret nothing)

The title of Edith Piaf's song dedicated to the French Foreign Legion

Chapter 1

The Charisma

'For over a hundred years the Legion has been a forerunner of a United States of Europe.' From a Legion recruiting pamphlet, 1954.

No military force in history has so vividly succeeded in stirring men's minds and imagination as the French Foreign Legion; no force has been so universally known and none has been invested with such a wealth of charisma. If ever there was 'romance' in war then the Foreign Legion has epitomized it.

I asked a group of people to write down, spontaneously, what the Foreign Legion means to them, and certain words and phrases recurred so frequently as to be standard: adventure, glamour, never surrender, toughness, brutality and torture, 'march or die', desert fighting, *esprit de corps*, pride, ruthless sergeants.

I asked the group their conception of legionnaires as men and, again, standardized replies. They are 'men who have joined the Legion to forget (or escape)'; 'men without hope'; 'the scum (or riff-raff) of the earth'; 'men with a natural love of fighting'; 'ruthless mercenaries'.

To the military historian such visualizations are predictable; they are the product of wildly imaginative fiction, even wilder film versions of the Legion and of grotesque 'memoirs' either wholly fabricated or the work of malcontents and deserters unable to adapt to the unique conditions of the Legion.

Because of all this the Légion Étrangère is also the most misunderstood of all fighting forces, the victim of much denigration and defamation. The Legion's reputation is certainly spectacular—but mostly for the wrong reasons. The Legion of P. C. Wren and *Beau Geste* and of Ouida and *Under Two Flags* is not and never has been the real Legion. Ironically, fact is more intriguing and sometimes more bizarre than fiction. There are incidents in Legion history which many a yarn-spinner might hesitate to invent as too improbable.

The Legion needs to be explained before its history can be com-

11

prehended, so an analysis cannot start at the Legion's beginning in 1831 and proceed with simple chronology, even though its life span is short. Its traditional, effective life ended in 1962, but it lives still and is strong in numbers—about 7,500 in 1973. Because of the hiatus of a decade or so it is possible to see the Legion in clearer perspective than ever before, without the emotive interference of headlines proclaiming defeat or victory, virtue or degeneration.

Extraordinary and incompatible contrasts exist in the history of the Legion: for every word of condemnation a word of commendation; for every story of brutality one of humanity. Reduced to essentials there are two competing Legions in the minds of many people—the Heroic Legion and the Debased Legion. In the heroic version the Legion is made up of misfits with remarkable devotion to a cause, great loyalty to officers, *sous-officiers* and comrades; they are courageous, have fidelity and honour and are capable of great endurance. The contradictory version sees the Legion cruelly ill-treating its men, callously neglecting their suffering, underpaying them, brutalizing them and sacrificing their lives to save Frenchmen.

Both these pictures are over-simplified and misleading. How legionnaires felt about their corps in retrospect is pertinent. For instance just after World War II the Legion HQ in Sidi Bel-Abbes received a letter from a German, George Bohnert, living in the Rhineland who was seventy-six and about to die. He had served twenty years in the Legion and wrote, 'I wish to be buried in the folds of the flag, blue, white and red, and taken to my grave by a detachment of the Legion.' He had his wish and the letter is exhibited in the Legion museum.

Another legionnaire, William Holl, dying in Chicago, asked that his ashes be sent to Sidi Bel-Abbes, where the museum curator placed them in a wall cavity behind the plaque:

> Ici reposent les cendres de l'ancien Légionnaire
> William Holl
> Dont le dernier désir a été de reposer
> A la Légion.

The Legion's denigrators would say that most ex-soldiers remember only the best part of their service careers and become maudlin about it in old age. But some serving legionnaires are just as sentimental, like the Belgian sergeant who said simply in the early 1950s, 'The Legion is beautiful.'[1] The veteran *Daily Mail* correspondent, G. Ward Price, who spent much time with the Legion in Morocco during the 1920s and 1930s, wrote, 'It is a grand regiment—embodying the finest qualities of one of the world's most ancient but now gradually

12

disappearing figures, the professional soldier. And yet my advice to would-be legionnaires is: *Stay so.*[2]

Ward Price thought that to find a parallel to the institution of the Foreign Legion it would be necessary to go back to the Middle Ages. 'The knights of Malta, drawn as they were from many different nationalities, must have had the same sense of identification with a brotherhood of arms, transcending all ties of birth and language.' He believed that in their case, as with the Foreign Legion, this bond was constantly intensified by the experience of war dangers confronted in common, and feats of arms in which the glory was shared by all.

A soldier could be both critical of the Legion yet quick to resent criticism made against it, as was Legionnaire Perrott-White. 'From the moment I saw these things [the museum relics of the Legion], although no one has criticized the Legion more than I, I was fiercely jealous of the Legion's reputation.' [3]

Major Zinovi Pechkoff—son of Maxim Gorki—one of the great Legion figures, who understood the ordinary legionnaire as few other men did, was more spiritually poetic. 'In the Foreign Legion, as in the monastery, is realized the saying, "Whosoever will lose his life ... shall find it", and one may add, "Whosoever will lose his name ... shall find it".'[4]

Pechkoff's likening of the Legion to a monastic brotherhood is apt enough, because it did become a lay military order serving a flag with the zeal of priests dedicated to a crucifix. Pechkoff believed that the Legion could well serve as a model for mankind.

'Life will become wonderful when men finally realize the oneness of the human race, when all humanity will live as one harmonious whole. It is only through labor and effort that the darkness of ignorance, hatred and division will disappear. And it is only through work that mankind will be purified and raised from its narrow egotism. Here is a group of men representing twenty different nationalities which have been separated by enmities and strife. A common aim is given them, a useful piece of work set before them, and at once they become brothers in arms and companions in work.'

In fact men of at least eighty nationalities have served the Legion; and it must be understood that they primarily served the Legion and only by association served France, which many of its members hated. Legionnaires certainly do not fight for the *French*. They fight for the Legion, which is its own ideal. Nominally they fight under the French flag, and the men's pay, food, clothing and equipment are provided by the French Government, but they would probably

13

serve with equal zeal any other government which paid, fed and clothed them.

Most military forces subscribe to the sentiment of honour and fidelity, which matures into a code of honour and an oath of obedience. In many armies this oath often provides the excuse for individual cruelty and moral cowardice. The Legion, however, does not require its recruits to take any ceremonial oath, and legionnaires do not observe a formal rigid code. However, the recruit agrees in his written contract 'to serve with honour and fidelity', and to serve unconditionally for five years.

This concept poses a moral problem with two inseparable aspects; the conduct of the legionnaire towards the enemy and his conduct towards the Legion—and France.

Legionnaire Adrian Liddell Hart ran his head into the Legion's philosophy when he sought an interview with his colonel to explain a 'misunderstanding' which had resulted in a sentence of eight days in the cells. Liddell Hart, with a courage or naïveté that would have seemed to his comrades to border on the suicidal, said, 'I demand to see the colonel right away to save embarrassment. This is not a military question but a diplomatic one. In these circumstances it is impossible for me to fight for France.'

'You are not fighting for France—you are fighting for the Legion!' the captain shouted.[6] The Legion is not an occupation—it is a life!'[5]

Legionnaires have been indoctrinated with this *esprit de corps* to an extent that has few parallels. Great effort was obviously necessary to weld together men of diverse racial, political and social backgrounds few of whom, officially at least, had any patriotic motives to fight for France. They were not asked to fight for France; indeed France is seldom mentioned in Legion orders or conversation. The Legion doctrine is *Legion patria nostra* ('the Legion our fatherland') and its motto is *Valeur et Discipline*. Over and over, generations of legionnaires have been told of the Legion's victories and even of its valiant defeats—*every* Legion defeat is a valiant one. No other kind is possible, for the Legion, by tradition, fights to the last man. The feats of individual legionnaires who have shown great bravery and endurance are ceremonially recited and their comrades urged to emulate them. The greatest infamy in life, the legionnaire is told and told again, is to let down the Legion.

Inculcation of this ideal can be seen in fulsome tributes, such as that of Legionnaire Frederic Martin in 1912. 'Frankly, I think the Foreign Legion is the finest fighting force the world has ever seen. Its value to France is not, however, to be measured by its value as a fighting force. The prestige of the Legion is so great with the

14

ordinary French soldier that it occupies much the same position in the French Army of today as the famous Old Guard occupied in the army of Napoleon, and the presence of a battalion of the Legion among a force of ordinary French troops will convince every soldier in that force that he is on the winning side. A man or a regiment that can hearten up a force to that extent would be of incalculable military value even if they never fired a shot.'[6]

Legionnaire Martin's observation has been proved true many times, but the Legion always held an undefined status in the French Army. Not until 1931—its centenary year—was it included in the Army List, and then just below the notorious Bataillons d'Afrique penal units and just above the native colonial units.

Not all legionnaires were imbued with the *esprit de corps* exhibited by Martin. Less than twenty years later ex-Legionnaire 1384 wrote,* 'As . . . a Hell Hound in the pay of France, I accuse her of fostering and maintaining a fighting force the name of which, as she knows, must stink in the nostrils of decent men the world over. I accuse her of encouraging an organization which can only make inhuman brutes of men, which spreads disease, destruction and death wherever it moves. . . . The Legion is beyond plausibility. It is beyond ordinary human conception. It stands out as a thing apart from any other sort of activity in life as we know it today.'

Another man who claimed Legion experience, J. M. Armstrong, agreed with No. 1384. 'In the Legion, from the very beginning, you are scientifically and expertly humiliated in every way. You are just mud, lower than the lowest criminal sent to Devil's Island. The Foreign Legion has the reputation of being the hardest fighting, longest marching machine in the world. If this is true, and I have sometimes doubted it, the result is achieved not by encouragement to do your best but simply by making men so damned miserable that they just don't care what happens to them, or how long they carry on under the most wretched possible conditions.'[7]

Almost diametrically opposed were the views, at the same period, of 25292 Corporal A. L. Martin, 1st Regiment Foreign Legion, who joined the Legion on the advice of the Canadian Consul in Paris and never regretted following it. 'During the whole of my service in the Legion I never once saw or heard of a case of "brutality" such as figures so largely in the "memoirs" and other fiction written by

---

* The reason for this man's anonymity is puzzling since presumably the French authorities could have referred to his Legion number to find out who he was. If he enlisted under a *nom de guerre* he might just as well have used that in his book, *Hell Hounds of France* (in collaboration with W. J. Blackledge). It was fashionable at the time to condemn the Legion.

deserters, or by men who were discharged on medical grounds as soon as recruits arrived at Bel-Abbes. In the early part of 1931 many of us were vastly amused at a series of articles published in a north-country paper—"Twelve Months in Hell". These "startling revelations" emanated from a man who tried to join the Legion at Marseilles on September 9, 1930, and who was rejected for the "draft" for Algeria on the 26th of the same month, the intervening fortnight having been spent in a Marseilles hospital, suffering from jaundice.

'I do not say that brutality does not exist outside the Penal Battalion in Colomb-Béchar—only that I never saw a case. On one occasion I did see a sergeant kicking a Canadian, but as the latter had pulled off the sergeant's trousers and bitten him in the thigh, my sympathies were entirely pro-sergeant.

'The type of liar to whom I have referred above is responsible for the widespread idea that a recruit is at the mercy of devils disguised as NCOs, and that the slightest fault is punished in the most brutal and savage manner conceivable. There is no foundation whatsoever for such a supposition. It is infinitely easier to be punished, and punished more severely, in the British Army than in the Legion.'[8]

Martin's own instructor was a Persian with unique ideas on punishment; it was rare for him to send a man before the company commander, with the possibility of a court-martial and severe punishment. For flagrant breaches of discipline he would make a man clean out the lavatory with a tooth-brush on Sunday morning. Another idea, less severe, was to make a man clean fifty-six pairs of boots on a Saturday afternoon.

It might be as well here to dispose of those two arch traducers of the Foreign Legion—Louise de la Ramée (Ouida) and P. C. Wren, whose names are never even mentioned among Legion officers. Miss Ramée's master-tale of the Legion, *Under Two Flags* (1866), is even based on a false premise. Her classic hero, Bertie Cecil, was not a legionnaire at all but a trooper in the Chasseurs d'Afrique, which Miss Ramée apparently assumed was the same thing as the Legion. She did not know the Legion, but in compensation the passionate Miss Ramée created a great romantic character in Bertie, and she did know what went on in the minds of her characters; she has an Arab sheikh say bitterly to Bertie: 'To rifle a caravan is a crime, but to steal a continent is glory.'

Wren was not satisfied to have his novels regarded as romance; he insisted they were based on fact. For once the Legion was stung to rebuttal, but Wren stuck to his guns the way a legionnaire might hold the fort. Some of his novels are good yarns, but they have no validity as history. A few have no virtue as novels. *The Wages of*

Virtue must be one of the funniest Legion stories written—though it was not meant to be funny. A Russian legionnaire, Mikhail, is discovered by the brutal Italian legionnaire, Luigi, to be a girl. She appeals to Sir Montague Merline, posing as Legionnaire Jean Boule, for protection. Merline consults another Englishman in the Legion, Reginald Rupert; they happen to be father and son, though neither knows it. . . .

Wren did the Legion a great disservice with his statements that the Legion was drafted to tasks in the Spahi (native camel soldiers) barracks which the Spahi would rather die than touch; that Moroccan Goums were allowed to shout at legionnaires as they would at pariah dogs; and the 'joyless filles de joie draw aside their skirts from the infamous Legion'. Nonsense; many of those 'joyless filles' married legionnaires and lived happily.

Another lie-calumny which Wren helped to circulate was that French convicts were given the choice of Legion or prison. Frenchmen have never been permitted to join the Legion, though many have done so, posing as Belgian or Swiss.

Chapter 2

The Philosophy

'The Legion of the lost ones and the cohorts of the damned.' Rudyard Kipling.

'The legionnaire is an outlaw who has fallen out of the ranks of orderly human society, where he was ill at ease. He has a natural taste for risks. He wants to live his life. It is the only personal property left to him and he stakes it boldly.' General Villebois-Mareuil, 1912.

The Legion exists because there are always rebels, though this term must be used in the widest sense. Rebels of all kinds have found their way into the Legion—men who cannot tolerate a particular political regime, others who have become alienated from their own society and reject its values. Some have rebelled against the restrictions of domesticity and some against constraints imposed by law. A great many have rebelled against their own past and see the Legion as a new future. In effect, the Legion is sanctuary. The Legion's social mission, its hierarchy has constantly declared, is to redeem the lost and give new life to the hopeless.

It is not, of course, as altruistic as this. The Legion has declined to accept a lot of lost and hopeless men, but the idea has much truth and makes a useful recruiting slogan. But the Legion's greatest value to those men who have lost their faith, ideals, beliefs, trust or confidence in a former way of life is the anonymity the Legion confers on them. This is even more important than the food, clothing and shelter it gives them.

Since its inception the Legion has been aware of the psychological attraction of anonymity. It asked for no papers and accepted any name an applicant cared to give. Any inquiries about him were ignored, partly for convenience and because France did not wish to be accused of harbouring political agitators and criminals. In 1881 the Legion's maxim *Legio patria nostra* became official practice as well as principle. For foreigners the cloak and anonymity became complete, though sometimes agitation by friends—or enemies—

brought to light a Frenchman's membership in the Legion and he would be thrown out. In the early 1900s some legionnaires, with no guilty secrets, disliked the policy of official ignorance about their presence and deliberately sought publicity. Invariably they were punished, as much by their comrades as by Authority. After World War I the Legion became a little more selective in accepting recruits and began to fingerprint recruits at Marseilles to allow the police to check their records; serious criminals were not wanted. Then in 1931, in the reforms which accompanied centenary year, the Legion decided that if inquiries were made about a serving legionnaire the man's commanding officer could answer them—but only with the legionnaire's permission. This policy remained in 1973.

But while the Legion protects its men's secrets it wants to *know* those secrets, and one way or another it finds out. The new legionnaire, having told his story in Marseilles or Strasbourg or some other recruiting centre, thinks that is the end of it. But more interrogation comes when he is tired, hungry and demoralized on his arrival at Sidi Bel-Abbes or more recently in Corsica. 'So you come from Freudenstadt,' the interrogating NCO will say. 'Just point it out on the map. So . . . where *do* you come from?'

Or: 'You told the recruiting sergeant you had never been in France before arriving by train from Italy. But in your pocket we found a ticket from Brussels to Paris—how do you account for that?'

Such interrogation has varied in intensity over the decades, superficial when recruits were desperately needed, thorough according to the personal policy of the depot commandant.

On many occasions foreign governments, well aware that wanted men were in the Legion, angrily demanded their return. Legion practice has been to deny all knowledge of the man or simply to ignore the foreign request. As we shall see in a later chapter, the Legion has gone to extreme lengths to keep legionnaires out of trouble; political refugees are especially safe.

Despite popular belief the Legion *will* surrender a man to his government if its own senior officers are reasonably satisfied from evidence presented to them that he is guilty of murder. They take a lot of satisfying, and would probably surrender a man to the British police much more readily than to the Russians.

It is important in an analysis of the Legion to know why men join. Some have enlisted in desperation—better the deserts of North Africa and possible torture by Arab women or the jungles of Indo-China and death by disease than the cruelties of concentration camps. Some recruits are frankly materialistic and seek nothing more than shelter, food and work. The Legion has found that these are the potential

19

loafers and tends to discourage men who have no other motive for joining. At various times some men undoubtedly joined the Legion simply to drink, to sleep with as many harlots as possible and finally to die. All these desires could be achieved with terrible ease.

At least until France lost her empire some men joined for professional reasons, perhaps because they could not soldier in their own countries or preferred to soldier in the Legion. Until 1962 there were plenty of opportunities for action and for promotion.

Ten per cent of the Legion is made up of men who join for 'personal' reasons—so says the Legion itself. There is the adventurer, the type who wants excitement; there is the romantic, who finds satisfaction and perhaps inspiration in the desert sands or even in the jungle swamps of Indo-China or Madagascar. Both these types probably respond to the élan of the Legion. Without doubt there is the man with a broken heart, betrayed by the woman he loves and sparing no effort to make sure she knows to what lengths she has driven him. It is said that one man arrived at the Marseilles depot wearing top hat, white tie and tails, his heart broken at a fashionable ball by a girl who had rejected him. It could well be true. But at Marseilles' Fort Saint Jean men often arrived in such rags that they were given any kind of nondescript clothing—bowler hats, soft caps, capes, even kilts—until they were 'processed' and admitted as legionnaires.

A great personal loss—the death of somebody close to him—can drive a man into the Legion. Or the need to expiate some disgrace, such as dipping into the bank's till, or failing to pay a gambling debt, or seducing a girl, making her pregnant and so disgracing her. At the simplest level, some men merely want to *belong*, never before having belonged to family, group, community or society. It is possible to feel a deep sense of belonging, even of kinship, in the Legion.

Many a man wants to escape, but very few want to escape into nothing. A man needs to make a gesture, to exercise his ego and will. Some men escape into a religious community, not to become faceless but to give themselves features. So with the would-be legionnaire and the Legion.

Until the 1960s some men who joined the Legion were such misfits that they had their faces tattooed with death's heads, snakes, Red Indian-like tribal markings and ghastly designs. Major Pechkoff saw a legionnaire with the word *Fatalité* tattooed in large letters on his forehead.

It is still remembered in the Legion that a legionnaire visited a tattooist who printed in one-inch letters on his right hand the word *merde* ('shit'). It had escaped notice at his medical examination, but later caused much embarrassment. He was ordered to wear a glove so as to avoid giving offence to officers when saluting. But he liked giving offence, often forgot to wear the glove and spent many a fifteen-day stretch in prison. One legionnaire hated his captain, a French royalist, and had *Tread on the Lily* (of France) tattooed on his chest as a daily insult.

Perhaps men saw this form of exhibitionism as insurance against their ever returning to the ordinary world. The Legion had no official objection to grotesque tattoos until the training camps were moved to Corsica in the 1960s; it was then considered undesirable to have such hideously marked men under public scrutiny by tourists.

The Legion has had its intelligent, educated men. Its ranks have included high-grade bankrupts, clergymen who had disgraced their calling and other men trying manfully to redeem pride and honour. Most could easily have become *sous-officiers*, but they disdained promotion—a pity, for this would have completed the treatment. Without the responsibility they really needed some of these legionnaires quietly committed suicide.

A legionnaire with twenty years' service told me that no matter what reason a man chooses to give for joining the Legion it was an irresistible despair that made every one of them walk into the recruiting office. There was, he said, 'a period of mental agony' which preceded the decision to join and that this agony, shared by all, gave the Legion its cohesion and was the root of its camaraderie. This man had not read André Maurois, but no less a literary figure gave some thought to the psychology of legionnaires and drew these conclusions: 'All civilizations have their sufferers. In every country in Europe, and without doubt in America also, live men for whom life is a penance. Some of them have been stricken down by misfortunes or by unforeseen happenings, and the sight of the place: where they have been unhappy has become unbearable for them. Others have suffered by their own mistakes or they have committed some act for which their consciences reprove them; they know that they can reconstruct themselves only by escaping from their pasts. For all those beings, for all those whom Dostoyevsky calls the "Insulted and the Injured", the Foreign Legion offers a refuge.'[9]

Officially there are no nationalities in the Legion and every legionnaire must learn French; it might then be supposed that the martial qualities of each race would become fused, but Legino officers and some close observers of the Legion make pointed distinctions. One general agreement is that the Germans, because of disciplined tenacity, provide a solid nucleus for regular infantry defence; that the French (posing, of course, as Belgians or Swiss)

21

are at their best when flamboyant gallantry by individuals or small groups is given scope. Throughout Legion history the French have been the least and nastiest of legionnaires because there is less reason for them to be in the Legion at all. Since France is their home it follows that they must sink very low before reaching the point of desperation which takes them into the Legion. The scum of the Legion was, for much of its history, mostly French. Corrupt, violent, sadistic, they came from the gutters of Marseilles and Montmartre.

Officers have said that the Spaniards display fanatical bravery in assault and hand-to-hand fighting, while the Italians are clever in avoiding danger. But some Legion officers can find instances to disprove all these assertions and assumptions. One officer of thirty years' service swore to me that the Hungarians are the staunchest and the Poles the most courageous. The British, it seems, are the least likely to become assimilated into the Legion but the most likely to assume command when officers and NCOs are killed or wounded in action. Americans, this same officer told me, are not 'legionnaire material'. Once they discover the Legion is not some kind of game like American football they want to get out.

But if Americans want to get out—and some have pulled powerful strings to do so—the best graduates from St Cyr, the French military academy, want to get in. To be an officer of the Foreign Legion carries high military and social status, and the Legion for many years has had the privilege of scooping the cream of each year's St Cyr output. Contrary to another misconception it *is* possible for foreigners to gain a commission in the Legion and many have done so.

Critics of the Legion say that the suicide rate, certainly a high one at times, indicates poor leadership. But these men had already committed a kind of moral suicide by renouncing their backgrounds. When posted to desolate desert outposts for long periods or when on tedious, monotonous duties they developed melancholia—the dreaded *cafard*—which, in extreme cases, led to suicide. Drink was an aggravating factor.

At least since World War I Legion officers care for their men to a degree unknown in most armies, and infinitely more than in the French Army itself. The Legion officer calls his men 'Mes enfants' —and he means it. Tales of leaders deliberately leaving men to die in the desert are pure fiction. One ex-legionnaire, building up a picture of officer brutality, relates an incident in a campaign against the Riffs. A legionnaire fell from the ranks in exhaustion. An officer immediately ordered his comrades to strip him to the skin, take his rifle, kit and water-bottle and leave him. And, so his story goes, they did so. It is too much to believe either that the officer would give such an order or that legionnaires would obey it. Officers did not make such decisions even during desperate retreats. The legionnaires' own tradition of 'March or die' has appeared to give veracity to the legend—and men did die on the march. They fought in cruel climate and terrain, marched long distances and carried heavy weights, but the camaraderie which invested the Legion would never have permitted a man to be left alone to die. Sometimes a whole section or platoon died, but that was a very different matter.

Another misconception is that the very fact of being a legionnaire somehow makes a man courageous. This is not so, but training, indoctrination, inculcation of Legion tradition—all this has given groups of legionnaires a corporate will to hold on against impossible odds. Responsibility is a strong inducement for courage; officers and NCOs can more easily be brave than their private soldiers. But it is interesting to note that many men who had won great distinction as officers in their own armies—German, Italian, Russian, for instance —were failures as legionnaires. They no longer had the preoccupation of special duties or responsibilities or the crutch of living up to what was expected of them.

The various characteristics which form the Legion amalgam have prompted some writers to speak of the 'mystique' of the Legion, a facet which the veteran Pechkoff could not see at all. Rather than mystique the Legion's principles were simple fact to him, and he wrote about them as absolutes and truisms. One evening in the blue shadows of the Moroccan mountains he wrote, 'We are the pioneers who open a new country. We are the rugged, primitive labourers who do the hardest work. We are the visionaries who see wonderful possibilities in the future. After the Legion, other men will come. These men will be praised. Their names will be known. But it is our men of the Legion who have paved the way with their untiring labour. Every path we have bears the pain of our men. It is they who have opened the way for civilization to come into the heart of this savage country. I like this primitive life, I feel so strong and gay. I feel in communion with my men.'[10]

Such a communion was practical as well as spiritual, because from the outset the French Government made it clear that the Legion must fend for itself in many respects. This produced the most common Legion maxim—'Tu es Legionnaire; démerde-toi (or démerdez-vous)'. Freely translated, this means, 'You're a legionnaire; all right, fend for yourself. Get yourself out of the mess and don't expect a helping hand.'

A *bleu*, or new recruit, arriving at a barracks might ask the officer who addressed the draft, 'Are we going to be taught French?'

'Démerde-toi!' would be the instant reply. At various times the Legion made attempts to organize the teaching of French as part of the training, but it did not work. Survival meant learning French, and even the most unwilling of legionnaires soon had a working knowledge of the language.

Another practical expression of communion is the tradition which demands that legionnaires stand together in any adversity, not merely in armed conflict. Its manifestation is the cry 'À moi la Légion!' ('To me the Legion!'). Legionnaires were always unpopular with native inhabitants, colonial troops and even with French troops, so not infrequently a lone legionnaire or a small group would be attacked in side streets, bazaars or bars from Mexico to Indo-China. In such a predicament the legionnaire had only to yell 'À moi la Légion!' and every legionnaire within earshot would echo the cry and rush to help. It has been known for as many as five hundred legionnaires to answer a single cry for help, with dire results for the assailants. The same call was used in battle, usually by leaders but often by a lone legionnaire in a tight corner.

No holds are barred after that cry—'À moi la Légion!' In the early 1920s a sergeant of the Legion intervened in a quarrel in Algiers between some legionnaires and criminal types of the Bataillon d'Afrique. In the scuffle a young thug of the *Bat-d'Af* put a hand grenade, pin drawn, into the sergeant's pocket. The explosion blew him to pieces. Within half an hour every *Bat-d'Af* who could be found was being savagely attacked; the streets were littered with badly injured men. Six soldiers of the Bataillon d'Afrique were killed, and to prevent further bloodshed the legionnaires were confined to barracks for three days and then moved to another post.

Whatever the degree of officer-soldier communion Pechkoff and others felt, the legionnaire was often the victim of the démerdez-vous principle during his five years' service. It was commonplace in the Legion's colonial days for a group of legionnaires to be dumped on a piece of waste ground and told to build a house or depot. Nobody gave them any tools or materials or advice. But the house was built.

The trouble was that the Legion became all too proficient at fending for itself so that the Government rarely granted credits for building purposes. When the Legion settled in at Sidi Bel-Abbes they were expected to do so without financial, material or architectural help from home. Gradually the Legion built itself two vast groups of barracks, a magnificent swimming-pool and two-thousand-seat cinema and much else—entirely with the hands of the legionnaires and without French Government money.

But the Government does give something in return for the legionnaire's blood and sweat, his anguish and frustrations. At the end of his five-year contract, provided he has committed no serious crime, he may apply for French citizenship and will almost certainly be granted it. 'Legionnaires are French, not by the blood of their birth, but by the blood they shed for France,' as the Legion so poetically puts it. The amount of blood must make the gods weep.

Chapter 3

Discipline and Punishment

'No soldiers who are perpetually abused, mistreated or overworked could rise to the splendid state of discipline which is characteristic of the Legion and without which it could never have achieved the battle honours which are its pride.' Captain George Fielding Eliot, military correspondent of the *New York Times*, in the *American Military Journal*, April 1928.

It is obvious that discipline must be firm to mould a large group of tough men from many nationalities into a fighting force capable of survival against brutal enemies and harsh terrain and climate. Officers and *sous-officiers* were dealing with many men who had no inner discipline and resented all forms of authority, with others who had held high rank in their own armies and were naturally not inclined to take orders from men they considered their military and social inferiors. As the French Army commanders began to realize what the Legion could achieve the more they *expected* it to achieve, and even more discipline was required.

Unfortunately for the reputation of the Legion its disciplinary methods were the focus of sensational novelists. Also men who could not take the hard life and deserted wrote bitter indictments of Legion discipline and punishment, forgetting that it was precisely this discipline which might have saved their lives in some encounter. Other legionnaire writers concede the need for stern disciplinary measures.

It is true that some officers and *sous-officiers* became martinets and inflicted cruel punishments. But the men always had a form of insurance against the brutality of superiors. A *sous-officier* could be reduced to the ranks for a wide variety of offences and, had he been cruel in his higher rank, his life as an ordinary legionnaire was intolerable. It was always easy enough in the excitement of an action to shoot a harsh officer or non-commissioned officer.

Some stories of punishment can be readily substantiated; others are impossible to verify. The investigator can only offer a professional opinion as to their veracity. One legionnaire I have no difficulty in

26

believing is Perrott-White, who had a good record in the British Army before he joined the Legion prior to World War II.[11] He saw an old legionnaire strung upside-down between two posts with his head just off the ground for seven hours. Sometimes, he says, a man would be forced to lie for a week under a tent on a floor consisting of sharp stones and would receive only bread and water twice a day. In another punishment he describes, a man was spread-eagled to a tree or a wagon wheel in the blazing sun and occasionally doused with water.

Perrott-White found some justification for these punishments. 'When dealing with some of the types of men we had in the Legion, such brutality may have been necessary, for they did not respond to any other treatment. A little brutality at the right time might possibly contribute to saving their lives in the future.'

An earlier punishment, described by Carlé[12] and other legionnaires, was the 'silo', a funnel-shaped hole in the ground, broad at the top and narrowing to a point at the bottom. A man could neither stand nor lie down in it, but must half crouch in his own excrement through the heat of the day and the cold of night.

Early in this century General Négrier, making a surprise inspection of the barracks at Saida, found a row of fifteen silos, all occupied by prisoners. Angrily he ordered the men released, the holes filled up, and an end to that form of punishment in the Legion.

Even more brutal was the *crapaudine* treatment. *Crapaud* means toad in French, and a man subjected to the punishment found himself in the shape of a toad, lying on his belly, his wrists and ankles lashed tightly behind his back. The torture of having circulation cut off sometimes drove men insane. The *crapaudine* was used freely as a field punishment in the French Army before Jacques Londrés exposed various forms of cruelty in the Army's disciplinary measures. Officially it was stopped in 1920, but it persisted for years afterward in the Legion's penal battalion.

An English legionnaire, George Manington, wrote in 1907, 'Much has been said concerning the iron discipline which reigns supreme in the Legion, but whilst serving with the corps I never suffered any real inconvenience from it: unless a punishment of "two days to barracks" can be considered of much account. It was well merited, for, through sheer carelessness, or perhaps because I wanted to get out a little sooner, I forgot that I was orderly man for the day, and left all the tin platters in the room after the evening meal was finished, instead of taking them down to the cook-house.'[13]

A German, Legionnaire Ernst F. Loehndorff, who served in the Legion during the 1920s, writes in terms of savage indictment and professed to see no humanity in the Legion—'this blot of shame on the world'.[14] At one time he spent several months at Fort Jonnart, a desert post 'when both men and officers began to act like caged beasts'. According to Loehndorff a comrade, Pieter de Gries, a Walloon, neglected to salute the captain, whom he had nicknamed 'Machine-gun', as he crossed the yard. As a punishment he was ordered to count one by one the contents of a big sack of dates. The Walloon looked at the commandant when he heard the command, his eyes glared, and he seemed about to attack the officer. Then he grunted: 'No!'

He was then locked up in the hottest of the cells, with chains on his hands and feet, while 'Machine-gun' walked up and down the yard for hours, stopping frequently in front of the cell and waiting to hear whether de Gries would whine or yell with rage or despair 'like his fellow-sufferers in the other holes'. Gries kept silent all that day and night. Loehndorff wrote, 'It is now midday again, a blazing heat streams down from the burning sky, pressing one to the earth and making one feel like a dried-up wash-rag. The Walloon is taken outside the fort, stripped and buried naked in sand up to his neck. His eyes had a mocking look at first, but became bloodshot, and after about half an hour an appalling shriek comes from his vivid lips. And while we stupefied legionnaires stand glaring at him, he yells for mercy without ceasing. He is willing to count ten sacks of dates, a hundred even, if only somebody will take him out of the terrible blazing heat that is burning and stifling him! The night is over. And the Walloon's spirit is broken. He now belongs to the Legionnaires who execute every command, be it ever so crazy, submissively and idiotically, with the greatest hurry.'

It was Loehndorff, too, who describes a bizarre episode at Sidi Bel-Abbes. At 7 a.m. one morning the yard was filled with officers and sergeants while small groups of legionnaires carried out various duties. Then from the prison block came a dozen or so men who fell into line not far from Loehndorff. 'With them,' Loehndorff wrote, 'is a small dapper sergeant with a fine, cold, bronzed face, and a small slovenly corporal in a horizon-blue uniform and a green bonnet. He has brutal features, flaming red hair, and a pink, freckled face, with a bulldog mouth and outstanding ears. A still more unfavourable impression is made by the soldiers who stand before these two like statues. They are clad only in long, thin linen trousers and the black-and-white striped shirt of the Legion. None of them wears the scarf or has any covering for his head. Their eyes lie deep in their sockets, surrounded with blue rings in their pale, emaciated faces. Many of these eyes express an impotent fury; the fury of wild

animals that fear the whip and secretly tremble before it. . . . Others
are lustreless and dim, while others again radiate such helpless
despair and resignation that I feel a cold shudder run down my back
as I sit silently looking at them.

'The sergeant gives a command, lights a cigarette, and leans
against the nearest tree, while the ugly little corporal, who looks like a
handy-man of hell, claps his heels together and lets a foxy, obsequious
smile play over his blubber lips. At his word the prisoners begin to
run round in a circle. The running trot goes on! At the word of
command they fall on to the sharp gravel, leap up and go on running
again. Trotting, always trotting! Their sides tremble as with worn-
out jades, their breath comes in jerks, their eyes flicker, glare, and
grow red.

' "Up! Down!" comes the gloating voice of the corporal, while
the sergeant, the real tormentor, leans languidly against the tree and
watches the scene with his cold, handsome face. He appears not to
be in the least aware of the wretches, whose lips are covered with
foam and whose tongues are hanging out. Twice . . . three times . . .
a wretch falls down, is unable to get up, and remains panting and
whining, while his companions in misfortune go on running. Each
time the sergeant wakes up out of his dream-world; he leaps forward, and without saying a word belabours the fallen man with
kicks in the soft parts till the poor wretch drags himself up with a
hoarse cry; and goaded by fear to make an almost supernatural effort
of will, he staggers along with the rest. Unable to stand the sight any
longer, I get up and hurry horror-stricken to our sleeping shed, where
I lean in the doorway and look back again. What have these men been
guilty of that they should be punished in such a way?

'I now observe that the tormented wretches are allowed to take
a rest, and I count exactly five minutes by my watch. Then the
torture begins again, while nearby officers in red breeches chat
unconcerned, and legionaries give the unhappy group a good berth
and cast a timid look over their shoulders as they go about their tasks.
The wretches now have to strap a sort of knapsack on to their backs,
after taking off their shirts. Then they begin their trotting exercise
again.

'Suddenly an old, blue-nosed legionary with medals comes and
stands beside me. I grip him by the arm so anxiously that he takes
fright. "What have they done, man?" I whisper.

'Under pressure he replies: "Overstayed their furlough or done
some other trifle that fetches from three to sixty days under arrest.
With bread and water or thin soup, because that fat fellow there—he's
known all over Africa wherever there's a Legionary—he cleans up

all the food before it reaches the others. And you're locked up in a pitch dark cell by yourself with nothing but a stone bench to lie on and a thin blanket the size of a pocket handkerchief at night, and in the daytime six or seven hours of penal exercises!"

' "What's in the sacks?" I inquire.

' "Sand! Thirty or forty pounds. . . . Look! He's going to make them do climbing exercises!"

'He points in the direction of the wretches. At the corporal's command they clutch the trunks of the acacia trees and, their backs burdened with the heavy sacks, they strive desperately to raise themselves, while the corporal speeds them up with his heavy foot.'

How much credence can one give to Loehndorff's story? It seems grossly exaggerated by the testimony of other legionnaires. Bennett J. Doty, an American serving under the name of Gilbert Clare, who had no great love for the Legion, conceded that *sous-officiers* were rough and that they roared a great deal.[15] He served in the ranks at the same period as Loehndorff and found the sergeants and other non-coms were martinets and bitterly critical judges of drill and training standards. 'They are of all nationalities, and in character, some are good and some bad. But in all my stay I never witnessed any real brutality, nor any sergeant of the type of Lejaune in *Beau Geste*. As a matter of fact that would be impossible in the Legion. A brutal sergeant would not live long in a hard-boiled outfit like the Legion. He'd be murdered in his sleep. I did know some, however, who seemed to inflict punishment upon their men for the sheer joy of it.'

Sous-officiers in the French Army are, in descending order, Adjudant-Chef, Adjudant, Sergent-Major, Sergent-Chef, Sergent. Very much below them are the Caporal-Chef, and Caporal. In the cavalry Sergent is replaced by Marechal-des-Logis and Caporal by Brigadier. I have avoided these confusing differences and in general have given officers their stated rank and called most senior NCOs *sous-officiers*. I have not discriminated between first- and second-class legionnaires.

The *sous-officiers* held greater importance and prestige than senior NCOs in any other army; legionnaires had to salute them and they could award minor punishment on the spot. Because many officers, especially the French, were content to leave so much to their *sous-officiers*, some of these men abused their rank and a few were brutal. They developed a superiority complex, the *sous-officiers*; they were the *élite* of the *élite*. In their mess men of the same nationality—*even* a group of Germans—would speak French as a mark of etiquette and status. And good French, no matter how heavily accented.

Nobody ever denied that a period spent in the Legion's penal battalion was painful and exhausting, but even here imagination has exaggerated the treatment of prisoners. E. C. Trelawney-Ansell wrote the memoirs of a South African, E. Duplesis, stated to have risen to the rank of captain in the Legion during the 1920s.[16] Legion records contain no mention of this man, who is said to have been sentenced to fourteen days in the penal battalion for possessing live ammunition in barracks. According to Trelawney-Ansell's story he and others were marched five miles through shifting sand, with hands manacled behind them and a chain running from their wrists to a mule-drawn wagon. 'Flies and insects settled all over our exposed flesh. My hands, wrists and neck were soon feeling like fire, and as if a million mosquitoes had been stinging me for hours. My eyes were clotted and clogged with flies. These beastly things crawled up my nose and in my ears. . . . The agony of that march, without a drink of water, covered with those loathsome insects, with throat and nostrils clogged with the dust, must be imagined. At last we came to the tents which made up the camp, surrounded by a barbed wire fence ten feet high, and also by barbed wire entanglements. Our guards made the mules break into a trot for the last two hundred yards and we stumbled through the gateway, to fall on the ground dead beat. Exhausted. Unconscious. The head-keeper there—a sergeant—was a pretty bad devil, but I must admit that he had some fine devils to look after.

'When I came to my senses I was being dragged along on my heels. My eyes, nose and mouth were full of sand. In this condition, without even a drink of water, I was picked up and flung into a tent. Here I was left. What seemed to me hours after, I got to my feet and opened my kit. Then in unspeakable agony I flung myself on my single blanket. Here I slept until I was roused by the sharp blast of the damned corporal's whistle. Men rushed out pell-mell and lined up. Stripped to the waist, we were marched to the scene of our labours. I was in a road-making gang, our work being to smash huge boulders into small pieces for use as road metal. Each man was given a huge quarry hammer and a pick. In addition, we each had two panniers fastened across our shoulders by broad leather straps. In these panniers we carried the road metal to and from the place from which it was collected in mule carts. In the Penal Camp absolute silence was the rule while working, and the man who broke this rule was caned across his calves by the corporal. Five or six stripes with these canes by a hefty corporal, who laid on with right good will, and the man could hardly walk for an hour afterwards—without the most awful agony.'

Still, even that was better than being run before the camp commandant for breaking the silence rule. That always meant another thirty days 'for gross insubordination'. 'We were worked from early dawn to sunset and worked harder than any slave of olden days. This long stretch was only broken at midday, by a rest of fifteen minutes. Then we were issued with a half pound of bread which we wolfed down, and a half pint of water to moisten our parched throats. Our evening meal consisted of a small basin of macaroni and potatoes, with a half pound of bread—dry as a brick—and a pint of water.

'The work was exquisite torture. Adjectives are easy to use, but there is not one that I know of to describe what we went through. Torture is far too mild. To make matters worse the work was done under awful conditions. Yet to rebel meant a term in the Penal Battalion of from seven to ten years.'

Significantly, virtually all the accounts of brutality lack any names of places or men, dates or other evidence which could prove them true. Also it is fact that all 'special punishments'—by which is meant excessive cruelty imposed by either an officer or *sous-officier*—were abolished by law in 1902. Some legionnaires have written of being savagely flogged, but the Legion never in its history resorted to flogging, though this was a frequent and prolonged punishment in most armies, including the British Army. A particular flaw in the case of Trelawney-Ansell's Legionnaire Duplesis is that by a decree of 1912 only the commanding general could send a man to the penal battalion.

Certain punishments were standard. *Pelote*—pack-drill in the British Army—was reserved for group indiscipline. Ordered onto the parade square in fatigue dress with full 40-lb. packs, the group would spend an hour—under the eyes and tongue of a corporal—marching, double-marching and crawling around and around. These punishments, used extensively during the training period, were to make it clear that the majority always suffered for the faults of a few. To a point this was psychologically sound, for in battle a few rash, undisciplined men could bring disaster on the section or platoon.

Sometimes, as a disciplinary or training measure, roll-call was in *tenue de compagne*. This is Field Service Marching Order and was another collective punishment. At the time of roll-call the legionnaires stood at the foot of their beds in complete uniform with boots and gaiters, greatcoat with the enormous red epaulettes of the Legion, pack containing complete kit on back, water-bottle full of water slung at the belt, needle and cotton stuck into the lining of the kepi. In the pocket paper, pencil and five francs. If a legionnaire did not have five francs and asked where he was supposed to get it, the reply was, as always, 'Tu es legionnaire; démerde-toi.'

A heinous Legion crime was selling of material and equipment, though the temptation was strong to legionnaires so underpaid in their first year. Frequent kit inspections uncovered offenders, who were then charged ten times the value of the missing kit and sent to the cells for fifteen days.

Some men told horrific stories of punishments meted out by legionnaires upon legionnaires and condoned by officers. One of the most harrowing is that recounted by Francis A. Waterhouse, 'ex-legionnaire' 1484. 'At Gabez, Tunisia, a young German received a safety razor through the post, but it was stolen the first night. Next day suspicion fell on an Italian, Bolandia, who had sold the razor to another legionnaire. The owner reported the matter to the lieutenant, who called a parade and ordered Bolandia, the razor's owner, and the buyer into the centre of the square. He quickly exonerated the buyer as having acted in good faith. Bolandia denied having stolen the razor, so, according to Waterhouse, the lieutenant left it to the men to decide what action should be taken. That night a Russian, Boloskoff, produced a bag and suggested that every man who believed Bolandia to be guilty would put a pebble in the bag, while those who believed him innocent should put some sand; nobody would see what each man held in his closed hand. When the voting was complete the bag held nothing but pebbles. The legionnaires kicked Bolandia awake and Boloskoff told him to leave Gabez and walk the 70 miles of desert to safety—an impossibility, as they all knew. Waterhouse declined to take part in what then happened. Under Boloskoff's leadership the men 'pulled up four trees' from which they made a cross. Then they crucified Bolandia. In the morning somebody reported to the lieutenant that a legionnaire had died—'Bolandia has been found nailed to a tree'. According to Waterhouse, 'the least hint of a smile broke on the lieutenant's face'.[17]

It is the story which should be nailed. It is another of those 'as told to' yarns—in this case to Roger Wimbush. No date is given and the officer is not named. It is inconceivable that a Legion officer would not himself pronounce a sentence and equally unlikely that *sous-officiers*, who must have known what was going on, would not stop it. Italians were not popular legionnaires, but it seems improbable that Bolandia had no friends who would object to his crucifixion. He was supposed to be asleep while his fate was decided —also unlikely. And how, one may ask, did Waterhouse know of the faint smile on the lieutenant's face? One legionnaire might stab another in his sleep—this happened when men went berserk with *cafard*—but such deliberate group murder was wholly improbable in the Legion. The most damning flaw in the story is that the razor's owner is said to have reported the theft to the officer. His comrades would have regarded this as more of a crime than stealing the razor. Stealing in the Legion was endemic. A man who found a legionnaire with some of his property would beat him up—if he thought he could win—and take it back. If the thief was too big for him the owner would sneak back his property or steal from somebody else—'démerde-toi'.

It was this type of fanciful yarn which convinced the world that life in the Legion was a murderous hell.

These men were no saints and they were guilty of every crime imaginable. But, unlike most other armies, the Legion did not consider drunkenness a crime; indeed, no legionnaire was considered drunk if he could get to bed, even if he had to claw his way onto it. Legionnaires marched drunk, fought drunk and died drunk, and to condemn them is to lack compassion for what drove them to drink. These men were as lonely as any on earth and drink was their only real refuge.

Wine kept the Legion going. It was cheap, light and deceptively innocuous. A man began to drink it as lemonade, simply to quench a thirst; he went on drinking to the point where it both fired and extinguished him. There was so much wine in Algeria at times that European growers poured it away in the streets. From Sidi Bel-Abbes the legionnaires would look towards the Thessala Mountains, and those of them who had been in those mountains would tell the recruits how they were 'mountains of wine', for the Thessalas were matted with vineyards. Any place where cheap drink was available became a goal. The legionnaire's favourite drink for many years was raw white Spanish or Moroccan wine laced with Pernod; he called it 'earthquake'.

Legionnaires of the 1950s found that discipline was still tough and that slight infringements could result in severe penalties. Colin John, formerly a gunner officer in the British Army during World War II, was a member of a section in which a couple of men began talking while marching to attention.[18] The sergeant immediately ordered every man to lie face down, with rifles across the arms, held in the crook of the elbows. The whole section then had to pull itself forward on the elbows; if a man's rifle touched the ground he went to prison for fifteen days. The distance to be travelled might be only 100 yards; it could be 2 kilometres. John saw a man who had dragged himself along by his elbows for nearly two hours; the sleeves of his battle-dress blouse were in rags and his shirt beneath it soaked in blood. But he had the poise to stand to attention and ask the sergeant if he might smoke a cigarette. Legionnaire John—he became a sergent-chef—must have seen similar punishments in the British Army, except that no soldier would be sent to prison for allowing his rifle to touch the ground. I have seen commandos endure without complaint punishment as severe as that which John describes.

Most legionnaires accepted stoically any punishment they were sentenced to receive; the Legion motto was, after all, *Valeur et Discipline.* They were proud of their discipline and most of them recognized the need for the punishment which helped to produce it. Indeed it gave them a strange pride. There is a story of a legionnaire brought before his captain for punishment and the officer was scathing in his comments. The legionnaire said, 'I have done a bad thing and I deserve fifteen days' solitary, but take back, my captain, what you said about my being a criminal like a *Bat d'Af* man. I am a legionnaire.'

The reaction of the upper-class Englishman to being disciplined was something that Legion officers could never quite comprehend. An interesting illustration is that of Adrian Liddell Hart, son of Sir Basil Liddell Hart, the military historian. Hart joined the Legion for reasons not made too clear in the subsequent account of his experiences.[19] What stands out is his Britishness in the P. C. Wren tradition. Fined and punished for losing a shirt, Hart said to his officer, 'If you attach so much importance to it I will be glad to arrange for several nice new shirts to be sent from England.' The Legion sent him to Indo-China, where he was charged with insubordination. His CO told him he would go to prison. Hart again became very British. 'If you send me to prison there will be trouble for you and the French authorities.' A more senior officer then told him, 'We can't afford to have an international crisis every time you have a misunderstanding.' Hart's attitude probably illustrates why the Legion has always felt that it is not made for British or Americans.

If anyone might be expected to take a critical view of conditions in the Legion it would be a legionnaire's mother, and especially the mother of an American legionnaire. Son of a French father, Jean de la Chesnaye-Roeder, aged twenty-four, enlisted 'for adventure' in 1929. His mother, formerly Daisy Kirk, a member of a wealthy New York family, was anxious about her boy, and during the first two winters of his service stayed in Sidi Bel-Abbes, where he was stationed. This could have been embarrassing for Legionnaire Chesnaye-Roeder, but he did well as a soldier, was wounded in the spring of 1932 and became a sergeant in the 2nd Regiment at

35

Meknes, Morocco. Later that year Madame Chesnaye-Roeder made her home in Meknes to be near her son, who had convinced her that the Legion was the life for him. She came to know the Legion quite well and, irritated by calumnies about it, wrote to the *Chicago Tribune*:*

'Life in the Legion is not a life of luxury. It is hard, but it is a life that makes supermen. I have the highest regard for the Legion's officers. They are fine gentlemen and constantly concerned for their men's welfare. I have lived for many months in daily contact with Legionairies, with my mother's eyes wide open, and I can tell you that the outrageous stories printed against the Legion, especially in the United States, are libels that any half-way decent editor should be ashamed of.'

* 16th March 1933, Paris edition.

Chapter 4

An Appetite for Sex

Prostitute's Song
Je suis une putain des légionnaires,
Et j'en suis fière, que j'en suis fière!
(I am a whore of the legionnaires,
And I'm proud of it, how proud of it I am.)

An old Legion irony is that while many a man joins the Legion to forget a woman, every legionnaire can always join a woman to forget the Legion. All soldiers become preoccupied with sex, but legionnaires to a greater extent than most because they do not have the anticipation of going home on leave to wives and sweethearts or even to prostitutes of their own nationality. Many of them receive no mail from women to give them some vicarious sex-emotional satisfaction. Isolated from women for long periods, legionnaires became sex-obsessed and it is not surprising that sexual aberrations were commonplace or that brothels flourished in Legion centres.

Few respectable young Frenchwomen living in North Africa would have anything to do with a legionnaire below the rank of senior *sous-officier*. Every so often the Legion magazine *Kepi Blanc* runs an advertisement said to have appeared in a French paper many years ago.

J. V. bon. fam. jol. intel. charm. corres. avec légion pour allég. solit. mort. apport. fraîche dans sa vie combat. (Young virgin of good family, pretty, intelligent, charming, will correspond with a Legionnaire to brighten his solitude or death and bring freshness into his life of combat.)

Legionnaires appreciate the irony of the advertisement, and all have wondered about the identity of the legionnaire finally chosen by the young virgin from among the thousands of applications she is supposed to have received. Older, soured legionnaires are sure the advertisement was a cruel hoax in the first place.

The last time I saw the advertisement it was illustrated by a picture of the legionnaire as the girl sees him: Bearded, big, handsome and young—and then as he is, a rather nondescript, moronic recruit; and of her as he thinks of her—in a bikini with pneumatic breasts and a come-hither expression.

The French Army was always realistic about sex and for centuries allowed prostitutes to accompany the Army. It instituted the Bordel Militaire de Campagne—the ubiquitous BMC, or mobile military brothel—supervised by the Service de Santé, the health service. Some BMC units were set up wholly for Legion use.

Apart from the mobile brothel there were several remarkable institutions privately operated in Algiers, Saida, Sidi Bel-Abbes and elsewhere. Like the legionnaires, many of the Legion's girls signed a contract for five years, and some took with them as much as 2 million francs when they returned to France.

The bordello in Saida was built around a circular room about 35 feet in diameter; it had a glass dome, and a large part of the circumference was a well-stocked bar. A stairway close against the wall led up to a balcony which ran all the way around the room at a height of about 10 feet, giving access to sixteen bedroom doors, all painted in the Legion colours of red and green. As a legionnaire entered a room he would hang his kepi on the door, a tradition of this particular brothel. *Sous-officiers* paid twenty francs for the privilege and other ranks ten.

While the legionnaires had a drink at the bar, and covertly looked over the available girls, they could amuse themselves by studying the fresco, at eye-height, which ran completely around the room. It was an allegory depicting a man pursuing, capturing and seducing a woman; the woman, having been seduced, then bound the man to her with chains from which he tried to escape and in which he finally strangled himself.

This sixteen-panel fresco was the work of a veteran Russian legionnaire, Popov. In 1935 Popov had twenty days' leave following fighting service in Morocco. After three days he was broke and owed money to the brothel madam. Since he had sixteen days of leave remaining he offered to paint a panel a day for his food, two litres of wine and a different girl each night. There were only fifteen girls in the house, so he slept with the madam on the last night. Rumour has it that the Russian deserted and hanged himself a little later.

In Sidi Bel-Abbes the red-light district, so called because brothels had a red light over the door, was the 'Village Nègre'. There were Arab women in light-coloured clothing with silver bangles, and coins and glittering threads in their hair, blue tattooings on their faces, thick vermilion on their cheeks and tattooings on their calves. There were girls fifteen years of age beckoning with their henna-dyed hands; enormous Negresses against whose bluish-black skin the broad silver ornaments showed up sharp and dazzling; Frenchwomen, worn out and painted; Spanish women; and a few fair-haired Kabyle girls with blue eyes. All sat in a long row, beckoning and gossiping, or motionless beside flickering candles. ... To Loehndorff, this woman-market, seen from one end, 'with the various uniforms, glistening morass, shimmering, half-sunk stones, and the little pools of light around the burning candles, looks like a picture of demoniacal originality, exotically beautiful, and yet repulsive.'[20]

The legionnaire who wanted to spend a visit with a prostitute reported to the sanitary patrol, usually stationed at the entrance to the reserved quarter. His name was entered in a log book; on his departure he reported again and was given an injection supposed to protect him from gonorrhoea—*chaude pisse* in Legion language. If the man should contract gonorrhoea he would receive treatment at the nearest military hospital; but if he failed to register he went to prison for thirty days when the cure was complete.

Carlé's description of the Villege Nègre in the early years of the century is interesting. It was 'the home of every sort of disease and crime. In this narrow space the vice of Sidi Bel-Abbes was hidden. Songs and cries and shrieks filled the air. Before the huts women were sitting, poor prostitutes, who sold themselves for a few coppers and a drink of absinthe. Here was vice in its most primitive form. Modesty seemed to be a thing unknown. A Negress with a figure full of strength lay there stretched at full length almost naked; she was too worn out or too lazy to speak, she merely invited the passers-by with gestures to come into her hut. Near her a Frenchwoman, in whose face her awful life had cut deep furrows . . . beside her Arabian girls crouched, children almost . . . Italian women with the characteristic gold earrings of their race . . . Spaniards with oily, shining hair . . . they cried out to me from all sides in a curious patois of low French mixed with Arabic. The language of the legionnaire leaves nothing wanting in the way of force and clearness—the language of the Village Nègre was filth condensed. In the corner there leaned in a dignified repose an Arab policeman.'[21]

In Meknes, HQ of the 2nd Foreign Legion Regiment, the 'Quartier Réservé' was a small town in itself, supposedly the largest brothel in North Africa. It had about five hundred houses, divided into sections called the north and south villages. There were cafés, restaurants, dance halls and medical treatment rooms for men and women. The whole was surrounded by an 8-foot wall, with steel spikes and barbed wire to keep out unauthorized persons, and to prevent any of the women being smuggled into the city of Meknes. The only entry and exit were through the great steel-barred gates, one for each section. Just inside these gates were the guard-houses, manned twenty-four hours a day by the Legion patrol under a sergeant and a native regiment patrol. The corporal of the guard with three legionnaires and three native soldiers patrolled through the grounds at regular intervals and also looked into the cafés while passing. Every soldier wanting to enter, whether European or native, showed his barracks pass to the guard on the main gate, then passed into the reception room. Details of his pass were entered into a large book. He was then free to go where he liked, but on days with an even date only European soldiers could enter the north village and Arabs only the south village. On odd days the situation was reversed.

On leaving the soldier reported to the medical treatment room, where he was given prophylactic treatment and signed the register. The attendant issued a slip, dated and signed, which the soldier surrendered at the gate. Should the soldier develop venereal disease the fact that he had signed the treatment book saved him from severe punishment. All these precautions could not prevent disease, since a man could be infected before entry.[22] This whore-town was a Legion institution until the French left North Africa.

In Algiers the building the legionnaires knew best was a brothel —the Sphinx—one of the most remarkable bordellos in the world. A vast circular hall, five stories high with a glass roof, the Sphinx had five galleries which from the base of the building might, at a quick glance, have contained miles of library shelving. They were five galleries of harlots' rooms and cubicles. The Sphinx was not a purely military installation; civilians too could sip their brandy or gulp their beer as they watched the girls circulating. Most of them had come over from Marseilles and Toulouse, but during the Legion's heyday there were Spanish, Maltese, Sicilian and others. The man who couldn't find what he was looking for was hard to please—thin and fat girls, older predatory women, psuedo-prim girls, women with caked make-up, others with the fresh outdoor look. The veteran legionnaires got to know each harlot's speciality; the *bleus* had only to ask for what they wanted. The decision made, the bargain struck, up in the lift piloted by a small Arab boy to the girl's room. There was a certain variety in *décor*, but most rooms were lit only by a faint red light. Later most girls would escort a client back to the ground floor, dismiss him quickly and begin promenading again. There could have been few French soldiers who did not visit the Sphinx at some time; even at the most riotous civil war periods it stayed in business, if only because the FLN (the Algerian resistance movement) had its agents among the girls and hoped they would pick up some valuable information.

During the Moroccan campaign of the 1920s the BMCs were staffed mostly by Mauresques, with a few European women. According to Legionnaire Jean Martin 'every single one was the refuse of Moroccan brothels. . . . At Ou-Terbat they numbered ten or twelve, exposed to the fury of 5,000 solid young males, bubbling over with ardor and vitality. . . . But it was during the two or three evenings following the distribution of pay to the legionnaires when this institution became picturesque. In order to avoid bloody fights it was necessary to reserve one day for each corps: Legion, Spahis, *tirailleurs.* An imposing body of armed guards surrounded the BMC and supervised the adjacent area as well; on pay nights the guards made the clients line up in front of each tent where they patiently awaited their turn as if . . . at a bus stop. The sanitary service overflowing, the personnel was unable to exercise seriously the task of preventing disease.'[23]

Sex at a desert post took a depraved form, or at least required an abnormal sexual appetite. Occasionally a wandering Arab whoremaster would camp near Blockhouse Seven or some minor post and offer his grimy child prostitutes, little girls eleven or twelve years old, for hire. Or, in periods of prolonged peace, a Greek or Cypriot—the East's inveterate whore-masters—would wheel a couple of his women by donkey cart down the camel trails. The women, aging, ugly, and usually diseased, had reached the nadir of their trade.

Legionnaires in the remote desert seldom met the prostitutes whom they claimed to be the most beautiful and best in the world— teenage girls from the Oulad-Naïl tribe of Constantine, Algeria. These Kabyle girls had a century-old tradition of serving as prostitutes throughout North Africa. Some even followed the Legion to Indo-China, Madagascar and Europe. After they had earned enough money for a dowry they returned to their villages in Constantine, married local boys and had the reputation of becoming perfect wives and mothers.

Loehndorff spent more than six months at the oasis fort of Hadsherat-M'Guil, and saw 'a great quarrel' among the officers for first possession of an Arab harlot who appeared from out of the desert. Adorned with silver bangles, tattooed forehead, painted cheeks and with henna-red palms of the hands she had blithely wandered through a wilderness where any roaming nomad would have cut her throat for just one of the gold coins about her head. She stayed eight days; then, when the legionnaires had no money left, she went her way.

Loehndorff was honest enough to admit having bought the woman's favours. Most of the high-minded deserters who wrote their memoirs protest that they themselves were never more than voyeurs; no matter how exciting the 'unmentionable gestures' of the 'bespangled prostitutes of the lowest order', these legionnaire deserters, it seems, were never tempted. Some *exposés* of the Legion's sex life are written in terms of such naïve surprise or righteous indignation that the writers' previous years must have been remarkably sheltered. Francis Waterhouse, ex-Legionnaire 1484, seemed surprised when visiting a brothel that 'the girls made all sorts of proposals, many of them salacious'.[24]

The Legion was always a breeding ground for abnormal sex behaviour. The legionnaire's environment, the circumstances surrounding him, were such that a normal man's resistance to homosexual activity was easily broken down. Having to live in close proximity to scores of men of low moral standards only facilitated the process. The severe discipline, the adverse climate, deadly monotony, vicious influence and, above all, alcohol undermined the legionnaire's mental faculties and gradually weakened his moral standards. Homosexuality grew on him in easy stages.

Walter Kanitz, who served in the Legion during World War II, claims that love affairs among legionnaires were frequent, and the situation was tacitly accepted as normal by the commanding authorities as well as by the troops. No action was taken if these romances were exposed. 'Jealousy forms a major part of these affairs, and bloody fights among legionnaires for the affection of a "female" are so frequent that they are not even talked about. They belong to the normal routine of life in the Legion.'[25]

Sometimes jealousy led to murder. The regimental commander would punish the culprit, if his identity was known and if the murder took place within the barracks. If the jealous lover liquidated *l'homme fatal* of his love triangle in some dark part of the town outside the barracks the investigation was not pressed. The murder was officially put down to an act of some jealous or otherwise dissatisfied Arab, even when suspicion of the real culprit was strong.

Young recruits were constantly importuned by the more degenerate older legionnaires, and many a legionnaire's first fight was in defence of his virtue. One legionnaire is said to have shot himself after he had been outraged by a French officer, a suicide inevitable, as Legionnaire Carlé says, 'as he was the son of well-to-do parents in Saxony'.[26]

Many a legionnaire, waiting for the end of the fifteen years of service which entitled him to a pension, became 'engaged' to a prostitute who continued to work in the brothel, saving as much money as possible for a home after the legionnaire's discharge. Kanitz had a room-mate, a corporal, who was engaged to a blonde prostitute in Sidi Bel-Abbes. When he heard a legionnaire talking of making a visit to the Village Nègre he would give him a glowing description of his fiancée's charms and her skills, and insisted on taking the man to her. Nobody in the Legion considered this objectionable or even unusual. Many legionnaire-prostitute marriages remained stable and contented.

The Army, and the Legion in particular, felt very superior when, in the early 1950s, Marthe Richard persuaded the French Government to make brothels illegal, for the law applied only to metropolitan France. The institutions continued to flourish in North Africa and, with the BMC, were prominent in Legion life in Indo-China. During their stay in Indo-China the French claimed to have established the biggest military brothel in the world, though it was later eclipsed by the Americans when they succeeded the French in Vietnam. It was known as the Parc aux Buffles, the Buffalo Park, where thousands of prostitutes were available.

The BMC flourished as never before, largely because prostitution is considered an honourable profession among the Indo-Chinese. Every unit of battalion strength (about seven hundred men) had its BMC detachment. At each rear base in the Red River Delta there was a building in a secluded corner around which played the unit's eight or nine prostitutes in their transparent white silk trousers, while they waited for off-duty soldiers to come and spend fifty piastres.

The economics of the BMC were complex. Each was supervised by the Army health service and managed by a *maîtresse*, who served behind the bar and was responsible for discipline among her girls. She had to keep a strict account of money taken, for 20 per cent went to the battalion to be distributed to various company funds, while each Saturday the proprietress of the Central Military Brothel in Hanoi or Haiphong would drive out to visit the outposts and collect 30 per cent of the takings.[27]

Many a legionnaire—officer and man—made a private arrangement with an Indo-Chinese girl, Ammanites, Vietnamese, Tonkinese; these prostitute-mistresses were known as congayes (*congais*) and they and their men were broken-hearted when the French left

Indo-China for good. The legionnaires considered the girls of Indo-China the sexiest in the world,* but one legionnaire apparently thought they had a diabolical fascination and described it in a poem for *Kepi Blanc* in 1954. In translation it reads:

> Be not content with a *baiser* with the Congai
> Her designs are black
> Her breasts are yellow
> With black nipples.
> Touch not the cursed things
> For if she gives them to you
> You are lost.

If the poem was meant to be a warning then no doubt it was disregarded; legionnaires were lost men in any case. There were worse forms of being lost than in the arms of a gentle congaye.

* But the Americans considered sex with Vietnamese girls merely a higher form of masturbation.

Chapter 5

Le Cafard

'Bear in mind that the Foreign Legion is not, as you imagine, a gathering-place for rogues and convicts; rather it is the meeting place of your bad conscience, for in ninety-nine cases out of a hundred we are driven by bitter need, whether of the body or the spirit.' Legionaire Ernst Loehndorff, *Hell in the Foreign Legion.*

A word—and a malady—which will for ever be associated with the French Foreign Legion is *cafard*. The nearest printable equivalent in British Army slang is 'browned off' or, in the American Army, having 'the blues'. But these terms get nowhere near the emotion and fear, connotations and symptoms of *cafard*. Literally cafard is a beetle, but in the Legion it is the word which describes the effects of intolerable monotony and boredom. The *cafard* beetle crawls through a man's mind, destroying his will and ability to think rationally. Some legionnaires have believed that, literally, a loathsome beetle was crawling through their brain. More pathologically it is a collective name for all the crimes, excesses, stupidities and pranks which tortured nerves can commit. It runs the gamut from the depths of despair to the heights of madness, and its manifestations stretch from uncontrollable sobbing in bed at night to exhibitionism, murder, suicide—especially suicide—self-mutilation and planless flight into the desert or jungle. Sometimes legionnaires have torn off all their clothes and rushed towards the enemy, even towards Berber women, who were notorious for their depraved barbarity.

Educated men had a better chance to combat *cafard*. During Legionnaire Brian Stuart's time with the Legion—pre-World War II —30 per cent of legionnaires could not sign their own names and another 30 per cent could not read any language sufficiently easily to manage a newspaper or books.[28] Thus two-thirds of the Legion could do nothing to amuse themselves after training but meander about the towns, visit the red light districts and get drunk in canteens.

On active or inactive service at outposts there were not even these diversions. *Cafard* lay in wait for men without inner resources.

Erwin Carlé was one of the few legionnaire writers able to study the condition analytically. He found, through long postings to desert and mountain forts, that he lived in a state of continual irritation and that trifles enraged him. He saw men fighting over the daily quarter of a litre of the Legion wine as each watched with obsessional suspicion that the next man did not get more than he did. If one man was given a little more work than his neighbour in the barrackroom he shouted about protection and favouritism and sexual preference.

Carlé saw *cafard* make a legionnaire sit sullenly in gloomy melancholy for hours, speaking to nobody; if anybody sympathized with him he would respond with vile insults. A sufferer would run a bayonet through a comrade's body without any outward cause. 'The *cafard* is at its worst in the hot season when the sun burns down relentlessly from the cloudless, deep blue sky, with the strange greenish colouring peculiar to the horizon. Then the barracks yard of the Foreign Legion lies deserted. It is so hot that stones on the yellow, clayey ground seem to move in the glimmering, overheated air. Then in the infernal heat the *cafard* has often been the cause of great disaster.'[29]

Whole groups of soldiers could be affected by it in the same way. The legionnaires of half a company would put their heads together, planning some act of desperation. One time it would be mutiny *en masse*, at another time desertion in a body. The madness was well known wherever a company of legionnaires was stationed. In some form it was always present, even if only in that peculiar longing for continual change, that restlessness typical of the Foreign Legion.

Many legionnaires themselves were not aware of the influence *cafard* had on them. When an old legionnaire said grumpily, 'J'ai le cafard', he was telling his neighbours to keep clear of him, as he had a bad fit of blues. He had no idea that a madness was at work; the legionnaire could not foresee the effects of *cafard*. The typical '*cafard* demoniacs', the older, soured men who did their duty like machines and at other times hardly spoke at all, were instinctively feared, for their comrades knew that any moment the least trifle could lead to an outbreak of the madness. In some cases at least the madness led to farcical episodes.

In the early 1900s a sergeant was employed as clerk in the regimental office at Sidi Bel-Abbes. He had once been an officer in the regular French Army but was cashiered because of some scandal and had enlisted in the Legion as a Belgian. One day the colonel was unwell and confined to bed, and was visited by the sergeant-clerk, who had some papers for the chief's signature. The colonel was asleep when the sergeant arrived, and he was shown into the dressing-room. Here the sight of the colonel's uniform brought on a form of *cafard*. The sergeant thought that it would vary the monotony a little if he took a stroll round the town and showed the legionnaires their colonel in a new aspect—it was dark and the colonel was sick, so nobody would be surprised at his muffling up his face.

Half an hour afterwards a Legion sergeant, strolling along the tree-shaded Rue de Mascara, saw in the gloom the five-striped sleeve of the colonel's coat, and braced himself to justify his reputation as one of the smartest NCOs of the corps. His salute did not please his commanding officer this time, for the five-striped sleeve was raised in an imperative signal to stop, and an angry voice ordered him to return to barracks and take four days' confinement to barracks for slouching about the town in a dirty uniform and saluting his colonel in an unsoldier-like manner.

The 'colonel' promenaded the town for an hour, dealing out four days' arrest and speaking severely to every NCO he met, but complimenting slovenly legionnaires and calling them *mes enfants* with an affection that astonished them. He saluted parading prostitutes and generally behaved in a way that horrified the respectable people who saw him.

He now went into a dive where no officer had ever been seen before, and fraternized with some legionnaires he found there. Here he could not escape recognition, and the delight of the men at the joke reached such hilarious proportions that the café proprietor was alarmed and appealed to a couple of officers who happened to be passing to take their colonel away as he was very drunk and was creating a disturbance. . . .

In another case two legionnaires disappeared for a week and then marched into barracks, dressed as grenadiers of the eighteenth century, with tall, mitre-like head-dresses, blue coatees, red waistcoats, white knee-breeches and long blue-cloth gaiters. They had been nobody knew where, and with ingenuity and skill had fashioned these archaic uniforms out of their own.

Two other legionnaires, ex-officers of the Austrian Army, marched off southward one morning with their kits on their backs and their rifles in their hands. Brought back and charged with attempted desertion, they indignantly denied any such intention; they had enlisted to fight and, as the authorities had not carried out their contract by providing them with fighting, they went out to find some

47

for themselves. The CO recognized this as *cafard* and the men received only mild punishments.[30]

The *cafard* took a Belgian, said to have been an inspector of police, in a peculiar way. He committed burglaries and picked pockets for mere excitement. He certainly did not steal for profit, because he invariably returned his plunder after getting clear off with it, though he did this once too often and was caught.

In another form of *cafard*, legionnaires would suddenly go raving mad from too much drink and smash full and empty bottles over one another's heads in the canteen. Sometimes a man would fall down in a fit and, foaming at the mouth, beat about him with his hands and feet. Somebody would usually apply the dangerous, drastic remedy of squeezing the sufferer's testicles. The terrible pain generally brought him to.

Some legionnaires have feigned permanent *cafard* in an effort to be discharged as medically unfit, but this required great concentration and effort since everybody from the regimental doctor to the barrack-room corporal would keep him under observation for months. Loehndorff, who knew such men, considered that the torments a dissembler had to put up with were the equivalent of five years' service. One case puzzled him. A legionnaire supposedly mad submitted to the 'hunger cure' without a murmur and caught rats and mice; he would dance about with them during the doctor's visit and swallow them alive before the medical officer's eyes. But he was kept under observation because he had once been heard to say that he would do anything to get out of the Legion before his contract expired. Loehndorff was sure that only a 'perfect madman' could do the things this man did.

For many years the Legion has carefully watched for signs of *cafard* and the consequent risk of suicide, for suicide is contagious in an army. If a man kills himself unit officers and NCOs are strictly interrogated to find out why it could not have been prevented. Had the dead man shown no symptoms? Had he approached anybody for help, and what was done about it? Almost invariably after a suicide the dead man's section, platoon or company is broken up.

The Legion as a unit has manifestations of *cafard*, such as the *Compagnie hors Rangs*—the Company of Men Who Aren't There. In Algeria and other North African depots the Men Who Aren't There had a barrack-room allotted to them, with twelve meticulously aligned beds, all to their ghostly selves. There was a flesh and blood corporal in command of the room, and he was duly charged with maintaining good order and discipline. He was visited every night by 'Rounds'—the officer of the day— and, on being interrogated, replied, 'All well; so many legionnaires absent.' The *Compagnie hors Rangs* was made up of men who were out of Algeria on leave, men doing 'time' in the civil or military prisons, or who had been sent to the *Compagnie Discipline* at Colomb Béchar.[31]

Nobody in the Legion thought the practice was odd.

Chapter 6

Birth Pangs of the Legion

All without exception are animated by the desire to singularize themselves by the accomplishment of an exceptional task.' Legion lieutenant Jacques Weygand, son of Marshal Weygand, in his book *Légionnaire*.

The Légion Étrangère was founded on 9th March 1831 by a Royal Ordinance, a grand name for an unimposing piece of paper signed by the monarch of France, Louis Philippe. The legion was a creation of convenience and not the result of some romantic inspiration.

Before 1831 there existed a number of foreign regiments in royal service, notably the royal bodyguard, mostly Swiss mercenaries, and the Regiment of Hohenlohe (named after its founder) which had formerly been a unit of the Royal Foreign Legion, eight regiments raised during Napoleon's 'Hundred Days'; none had been ready to take part in the battle of Waterloo.

Under pressure to rule democratically, Louis disbanded all foreign units in his pay, but this left in Paris and other cities a large number of potentially dangerous men, many of them looking for any kind of trouble. With the French adventure in Algeria just beginning a thoughtful and famous soldier could see a use for these men. He was Marshal Soult, who knew good material when he saw it. And if this material was good it was also foreign, so nobody in France was likely to worry about their casualties or the conditions in which they lived. There was one stipulation: the Legion was never to be used in France except in case of war with a foreign country.

The idea quickly became reality. The men who turned up to join this legion of foreigners were asked no question about nationality or previous record and no proof of identity was required. The recruiters accepted at face value the name and particulars given, even when an obvious German gave an Italian name or a French-speaking Swiss swore he was Russian. This was the beginning of the 'no questions' tradition.

The first officer was Major Sicco, who commanded the recruiting depot at Langres. Sicco, though an able veteran, must have been startled by the diversity of ex-soldiers who flocked to Langres. He was appalled to hear from his sergeants that many of the 'foreigners' were French criminals and undesirables. He reported this to his superiors and ten days later the Government decreed that Frenchmen could not join the Legion. This was easily evaded; the French simply declared themselves to be Belgian or Swiss and there was no disproving their story. By this subterfuge Frenchmen have joined the Legion ever since.

Colonel Stoffel now took command, pushed the first battalions into shape and in batches dispatched them to Algeria, though the place did not acquire that name until 1839. The whole affair was so hurried that the French military authorities in Algiers were aghast at the build-up of what looked to them like a conglomeration of six thousand military scum.

To make matters even worse the Langres depot had sent invalids and cripples, men too old for army service and boys too young. Others had been lured into the Légion Étrangère on the promise that they could quickly become civilian settlers—all they had to do was make this known to the officers on arrival.

The few French officers appointed to command them had difficulty in making their orders understood, so the authorities resorted to two equally dubious expedients. They allowed the men to elect their own officers or gave command to men who claimed to have been former officers. This expedient, without proper reception facilities, and with liquor readily available in the North African heat, did not work. Much fighting, insubordination and drunkenness occurred. The only men to keep formation and morale were the former Swiss Guards and the Regiment of Hohenlohe, both of which had some of their former officers. They stood out like small islands of sanity in a wild atmosphere.

Colonel Stoffel selected some forceful French officers and with them forged the extraordinary rabble into some order, but it took six months. One difficulty was the problem of acquiring *sous-officiers* to train these men and impose discipline; few men from the French Regular Army volunteered until offered higher pay and promotion. Stoffel formed seven battalions, keeping strictly to the rule of the time that companies must be composed of men of the same nationality.

1st: Former Swiss Guards and Hohenlohe Regiment
2nd: Swiss and Germans
3rd: Swiss and Germans
4th: Spanish
5th: Mainly Italians and Sardinians

6th: Belgian and Dutch
7th: Polish

Stoffel worked hard, but these men were tough, foul-mouthed and without ties, so that discipline was a problem. The cells were usually full and punishment was severe. Because drink was cheap and plentiful—if they had no money the legionnaires stole their wine—brawling was frequent and often bloody. French officers and *sous-officiers* were sometimes beaten up.

Without a common language and with men of such varying intellect the Legion early developed a method of instruction which involved a minimum of talking and a maximum of demonstration and imitation, the whole being scaled down to the least capable member of the section. It evolved its own marching rhythm, a slow sixty-eight paces to the minute, but with the stride long to compensate for it. This is tiring to begin with, but it is well adapted to long marches over uneven ground, especially in hot weather.

Nobody in authority felt confident enough to commit the Foreign Legion to battle, especially as its desertion rate was high. The Algerians soon induced many legionnaires, by promises of money, wine and women, to fight for them against the French. Some French regular officers wrote bitterly that they had come up against small *units* of foreigners who were supposed to be fighting for France not against it. There seemed to be no unity in the Legion, despite the formation of national groups. In fact this was one of the principal factors militating against unity, though it had not yet been diagnosed as such; there was intense antipathy, often politically based, between groups of nationals.

Despite the apparent failure of the idea, in 1832 other recruiting depots were set up near France's frontiers to attract men from central Europe, Italy and Spain. Motives were not questioned, but the volunteers were more carefully examined for health, age and usefulness. In Algeria, despite the system of training now in effect and the tenuous foothold the French held in this violent country, the Army still hesitated about using the Foreign Legion as a fighting force. Instead when the legionnaires were not training they built their own camps and many roads and bridges, sank wells and put together rough but effective forts. The legionnaires could not know it but they were establishing another tradition—as nation builders. The growth of Algeria, Morocco and Tunisia—then merely one great area known as French North Africa—was largely due to the work of the Legion as soldiers and builders. The institution of hard work in the Legion was early established and slacking on the job was considered a punishable crime.

The French had not known what a hornets' nest they were entering when they decided on North Africa as an empire. With the spread of militant Mohammedanism the Arabs flooded in from the east, seizing many parts of the country, causing the Berbers, the inhabitants, to retire to their mountains. From this period there remained in Algeria both Berbers and Arabs and the country lived in a state of anarchy. The northern part of Algeria became known as the Barbary Coast. The brave but ruthless Berber pirates—the original barbarians—preyed on merchant shipping, provoking many Christian nations into sending punitive expeditions. In a complex political situation, the Dey—the overlord—had his seat in Algiers while various Beys, who were lesser leaders, governed various regions. All nominally owed allegiance to Constantinople, for Turkey held equally nominal control of the great region. Dey and Beys changed frequently as one adventurer ousted another.

France began to take an interest in Algeria in the 1820s and a quarrel followed when, supposedly, the French Consul was struck by the Dey in April 1827. A French retaliatory naval blockade was ineffectual, and the French sent an expeditionary force in June 1830. But it and other expeditions, eventually numbering thirty-five thousand, could do little more than establish a large bridgehead around Algiers and start to probe into the countryside.

Algiers was a French creation. The principal refuge of the Barbary pirates was a cluster of islands off the almost empty land that lay between Tunisia and Morocco. In Arabic the word for island is *el djezair*, the nearest thing to a name for the area. The French linked the islands for harbour works, turned El Djezair into Algiers and after a time called the land beyond Algeria.

Under pressure everywhere, the Army finally sent the 4th Foreign Legion Battalion to reinforce the regular garrison at Oran. But the 3rd Battalion, in Algiers, was the first Foreign Legion unit to be blooded. The Arabs had occupied a large building known as Maison Carrée, and the legionnaires drove them from the place on 27th April 1832. They held it as an outpost against several fierce attacks, but about a month later an officer and twenty-six legionnaires were caught nearby in the open by a large force of Arab horsemen. They fought to the last man and later their comrades counted seventy dead Arabs around the patrol. At the time nobody made any mention of seeds of tradition, but they were sown in that episode.

Colonel Stoffel returned to France in June 1832. He could feel proud of having established the Legion as a force of some repute. Colonel Combe, the new commandant, brought with him the first Regimental Colour—a mark of military acceptance. It was

53

embroidered on one side *Le Roi des Francais à la Légion Étrangère* and on the other *Honneur et Patrie.**

Combe stayed only briefly before handing over to Colonel Bernelle who, with strict discipline and efficient organization, further improved the Legion. The main French victories during 1833 were those of the Legion battalions, especially the Spanish units, whose men were more adept at guerrilla and irregular warfare than were the French Army units.

During the next few years the Legion battalions were used constantly, especially against the brave, ambitious and unscrupulous Abdul El Kader. In 1835 the French Army suffered two disasters at El Kader's hands—at Moulay Ishmael and Macta. Only the behaviour of the Legion units involved held French morale together. Without their efficient fighting rearguard action the French Army would have been wiped out.

While it was fighting so bravely for France the Legion was unaware that political forces were at work exploiting it. The Carlist war had broken out in Spain over succession to the Spanish throne and the French Government felt that some show of support for the Queen Regent was necessary. So to save their own troops, they *sold* her the French Foreign Legion—officers, men and equipment.

The Legion, five thousand strong, landed at Tarragona on 19th August 1835 to join the Queen Regent's supporters, the Christinos, and were rapturously received. While moving his units towards Catalonia Colonel Bernelle, no longer under French Army command, began to merge nationalities. The experiment worked well and, with irregular fighting experience in Algeria behind them, the legionnaires performed much better than the Christinos.

For more than a year they took part in a few battles and much sporadic fighting in the Pyrenean valleys of north-east Spain. Colonel Bernelle, too critical of high command for his own good, was relieved and replaced by Colonel Conrad. By now casualties, sickness, desertion and neglect had reduced the Legion to a parlous state. The Spanish, militarily inefficient at the best of times, gave preference in food, clothing, equipment and quarters to their own men, and the legionnaires suffered badly, many dying of cold. The Legion was forced to live off the country and thus became unpopular with the inhabitants. However, their officers, mostly French, worked devotedly to hold the men and their morale together.

When campaigning resumed in March 1837 the Legion was in

* Later the motto became *Valeur et Discipline*, which was retained until 1919, when the Legion was granted the old motto of the former Royal Swiss Guards— *Honneur et Fidélité*.

action on the plains of Aragon. At the village of Barbastro, four Legion companies and a Spanish unit were violently attacked by a Carlist army on 2nd June. This army in fact was formed almost entirely of a volunteer legion of mixed foreigners, so that soon Poles were fighting Poles, Italians were shooting at Italians and intra-national enmities flared to the point where the Carlist Legion charged with the bayonet. The French Legion stood firm and the close-quarter fighting became as fierce as could be imagined. In this exhausting death struggle Colonel Conrad, seeing his Legion waver, dashed into the battle and fell with a musket ball in his brain. After several hours' incessant combat the two legions fought each other to an exhausted standstill. The French Legion left the battlefield, so in theory the Carlist Legion won, but neither fought again in the war. The French Legion survivors, unpaid and neglected, were quartered around Pamplona where their only friends were their French officers. The Legion was formally disbanded on 6th December 1838, and the five hundred survivors returned to France the following month.

A summary of the Legion's activities in Spain—now so little known—can best be shown by their casualties. Officers: 23 killed, 109 wounded; legionnaires: 3,600 killed or died of wounds or sickness. Nobody knows how many were wounded but about 4,000 deserted.

Meanwhile another French Foreign Legion, of about eight hundred men under Major Bedeau, had been formed and was shipped to Algeria in December 1836. About four hundred old sweats from Spain joined it there and almost at once the unit was in action around Algiers, often forming part of the columns which marched into the mountain valleys. In France recruiting was intensified, and in July 1837 a second battalion was formed. Thus the Legion again officially became a regiment with a colonel in command.

The French politicians could make no progress in negotiations with the Bey of Constantine, so in October 1837 a large French force, containing a Legion battalion, moved out of Bône to attack the formidable fortress town of Constantine. This was to be the Legion's first major battle in North Africa.

The legionnaires were led by Major Bedeau, one of whose officers was the dashing Captain Leroy Saint-Arnaud, who would one day become a Marshal of France. He was thirty-six in 1837 and had left Paris in a hurry to escape from debts and scandals, determined, as he said, 'to become remarkable or die'. Despite chronic ill-health he was a natural military leader, and at Blida, in January 1837, had attacked Kader's troops and forced them to run. Saint-Arnaud wrote

55

to his brother at home, 'We have had our baptism of fire. The Legion has taken its place gloriously in the army and all the regiments that remained aloof from our foreigners now come to us and fraternize.'

But Blida had been a mere skirmish; Constantine was a major battle. After much intermittent but fierce fighting an assault was planned for 13th October. Significantly, when the units formed up for the attack, the Legion fell in some distance from the other units. Some French military historians have said that the legionnaires were already beginning to develop a superiority complex, others that the French troops had not yet wholly accepted the Legion.

The legionnaires led the way through a breach smashed by the artillery, crossed some streets under sniper fire and made for the main gate. Colonel Combe—a former commander of the Old Legion (the one sold to Spain)—led a rush on a barricade and was mortally wounded. The legionnaires stormed a second barricade, inspired by a Legion sergeant-major who seized an enemy flag. The battle was a 'near-run thing'—one of those fights ready to go either way, with both sides beaten. The defenders set off great explosions outside the walls and the French wavered. Saint-Arnaud rallied his legionnaires with shouts of 'Avanti! Schnell! Good luck! La Légion!' Possibly 'A moi, la Légion!' originated here with Saint-Arnaud. The men re-formed and were first into the city. Now Saint-Arnaud could write, 'Our Legion has made itself immortal. Our reputation is such that all other regiments congratulate us and we have taken our place at the head of the army.'

By October 1839 the Legion had four full battalions, including training units at Pau, southern France. Throughout 1839 and 1840 the Legion, as part of the larger French forces, was constantly in action, and in June 1840 about 1,200 legionnaires were left to garrison Meliana; for four months they fought off daily attacks, and suffered so severely from casualties, the heat and disease that when relieved in October only 288 men survived. In another notable incident a Legion battalion captured a rocky stronghold, the Djidjelli, were then surrounded and fought their way clear again.

In 1840 the whole French policy in Algeria changed. Now there was to be total conquest and total occupation, and General Bugeard was appointed to implement this policy. Bugeard, an able man, reduced the number of defended posts, introduced 'flying columns', guerrilla tactics and mule-carried mountain guns. He established the tradition of the *razzia*—the swift, ruthless, surprise punishment raid on offending villages. The French burnt crops, seized cattle and took prisoners. Sometimes they executed ringleaders. Kader was so badly beaten he was forced over the border into Morocco.

The Army hierarchy was now convinced of the Legion's usefulness, and it soon had two regiments—six battalions. The 1st Regiment, under Colonel Mouret, became a fine fighting force; the second was slower to reach this quality, though one of its commanders was Marie Patrice MacMahon, another officer destined to be a Marshal of France.

Bugeard had set up supply depots, known to the troops as Biscuitvilles. In 1843 the 3rd Battalion was sent to establish such a post about sixty miles south of Oran and just before the foothills. With some difficulty the battalion's officers selected the ground between the River Mekera and a mound dominated by the tomb of a marabout whose name had been Sidi Bel-Abbes, meaning Lord, the Happy One. This place was to become the most famous in the Legion's history as its base depot. The Arabs sensed its tactical importance and almost at once tried to wipe it out, but under an engineer officer, Captain Prudhon, the Legion built Sidi Bel-Abbes into a strongly fortified camp with permanent buildings. The Legion's ranks produced men who had been professional masons, carpenters, even draughtsmen. According to Legion records one company had five qualified architects. Among them these men built a town, including tall barracks in use a century later.

They were active years. The Legion, for a time, was in action against the Moors whose Sultan had sided with Kader. An action of 13th August 1845, when the legionnaires broke into a Moorish stronghold and killed 800 enemy soldiers for a loss of one of their own officers dead and 24 men wounded, ended Moorish aggression.

In April 1845 occurred an incident which was to give the Legion a bad name. A large band of Arabs, retreating before a Legion column, hid in some mountain grottoes. Saint-Arnaud, in command, sent in a legionnaire carrying a white flag asking them to surrender, but he was killed. Unable to get at the Arabs, Saint-Arnaud ordered the legionnaires to light fires to smoke them out; the Arabs stayed put, perhaps in fear of French bayonets waiting outside, and about six hundred of them were asphyxiated. This story was exaggerated to the point where the Legion was accused of having sadistically burnt thousands of Arabs alive. It has always been used by detractors of the Legion.

Nevertheless Saint-Arnaud *was* ruthless, and according to one historian of the Legion 'relished brutality'.[32] The Legion became known as Saint-Arnaud's 'Infernal Column'. He gave scant mercy to Arabs overrun by his troops, who ill deserved whatever infamy Saint-Arnaud brought upon them.

The French arch-enemy, Kader, was caught and exiled, but in

eastern Algeria the Kabyle warriors, inspired by the Bey of Constantine, were constantly attacking French posts. The French decided to extend their influence to the edge of the Sahara and a *bataillon de marche* of the Legion under Colonel MacMahon, and other units, reached Biskra, 'the Garden of Allah'.

A *bataillon de marche*, an *ad hoc* formation assembled for a special purpose, was one of Napoleon's ideas. His theory was that when such a task force was being formed each regiment would naturally send its best men to represent it, since unit prestige and honour were at stake. In the Legion the idea worked efficiently.

At M'Chounech three thousand tribesmen held a natural defensive position along a rocky ridge, and two French regular battalions twice failed to take the position. MacMahon called up the Legion battalion, briefly harangued them and sent them into battle. They crossed a ravine under fire, scaled the cliffs and in twenty minutes had captured the 'impregnable' position. Perhaps MacMahon had made psychological use of informing the legionnaires that the two sons of the King of France were watching them. The 2nd Regiment was awarded a Regimental Colour as a symbol of merit.

Actions of this sort occurred frequently in the Greater Atlas Mountains and on into the Sahara. One of the more prominent Legion exploits occurred at Zaatcha, a large group of palm-tree-covered oases near Biskra, in July 1849. A rebel leader, Bou Ziane, had cleverly transformed Zaatcha into a unique fortress. Criss-crossed by irrigation canals, Zaatcha had many strongly built houses, each within a walled garden and resembling a miniature fort. The first French attack failed, and even after several months' preparation a second attack was beaten back. With the Legion in the van a third attack on 26th October won through and Zaatcha was captured after desperate fighting. Bou Ziane surrendered to the Zouaves, who killed him. He would have been safer with the Legion, who respected courageous enemies.

Throughout the 1840s and 1850s pockets of Algeria fell to the French, except the mountains of the Greater Kabylia. Many French generals had their toughest schooling there. French colonists began to arrive, to spread as farmers into the occupied areas.

The Legion's early experience in the North African heat resulted in experiments with its uniform. In the hellish heat of the days it seemed absurd for a man to wear a long, heavy coat. But the men who cast off their coats soon found that they were exhausted on the march more quickly than men who wore their long *capotes*. They discovered what the desert Arabs had learned centuries previously: if a man dressed too lightly, the wind dried his sweat and the salt of his body was evaporated quickly, weakening him. So the Legion retained its long coat, though each legionnaire tried to obtain an outsize that fitted him almost as loosely as an Arab's cloak. The white neckcloth was attached to the cap to protect the neck from the beating sun. White duck trousers, such as the old Legion had worn in Spain, replaced the baggy red woollens—and white quickly became a dirty grey. Units in the desert also adopted the Arab *shech*, a muslin wrap to cover the face in sandstorms.

But the Legion was soon to embark on a campaign where they would exchange sandstorms for the misery of rain and mud. The Crimean War had broken out.

Chapter 7

The European Adventures

'Legionnaires, servez d'example aux autres!' General Canrobert to the Legion in battle in the Crimea, 1854.

It had been originally decided that the Legion would not fight in European wars because of political objections, but when the Crimean War broke out Saint-Arnaud, now a general, realizing the toughness of the campaign, asked for three battalions of the Legion. He got them after fierce argument. As the Brigade Étrangère, this unit suffered badly from a cholera epidemic before becoming part of Canrobert's division, the best of the French force.

The Russians called the legionnaires 'Leather Bellies' from the leather waist belt and cartridge belt worn squarely on the front; they were the only French Army troops to wear this gear.

Their behaviour during the battle for the Heights of the Alma, 1854, impressed Canrobert, and he used the brigade again during the siege of Sebastopol, 1854–5. The Legion lost 72 officers and 1,625 legionnaires killed and wounded, apart from sickness casualties. Yet the legionnaires survived better, suffered relatively less and had higher morale than other formations. Using debris for which other soldiers could find no use they produced ovens, stoves and other heating devices during the dreadful winters. When the Brigade Étrangère entered Sebastopol, General Bazaine, a former sergeant in the Old Legion, was nominated as commander. As a reward for services rendered the French Government decreed that all foreigners who had fought for France—six of the eight Legion regiments had fought in the Crimea—could become naturalized Frenchmen and could serve in French regiments if they wished. Many legionnaires took advantage of the opportunity to become French—most were stateless anyway—but few opted out of the Legion.

'The war in the Crimea,' wrote Colonel Villebous-Mareuil, 'could not but show vividly the great military valour of the troops in the Foreign Legion. In this terrible campaign, where the endurance, the various aptitudes, the innate bravery of our army are prodigious, the legionnaires have forged for themselves an outstanding reputation.'

After the Crimean War the Legion bandmaster, Wilhelm, composed the stirring slow march which has been the principal Legion march ever since. Its title is 'Boudin'—which means 'black pudding' or 'black sausage'. The words of the chorus are about this food.

Tiens, voilà du boudin, voilà du boudin, voilà du boudin!
Pour les Alsaciens, les Suisses et les Lorrains.
Pour les Belges n'y en a plus; pour les Belges n'y en a plus!
Ce sont des tireurs au cul.
('Look, here's some sausage, here's some sausage, here's some sausage,
For the Swiss and the lads from Alsace-Lorraine.
But there's no more for the Belgians, there's no more for the Belgians,
Because they're just a lot of shirkers.')

Nobody knows why Wilhelm excepted the Belgians for a sausage issue, but many thousands of Belgian legionnaires have lustily shouted this song without feeling offended. It seems remarkable that a tune on such a theme could produce the heroism it did. A special ritual accompanies 'Boudin' when sung in the officers' mess. The most junior officer stands, looks his CO in the eye and commands 'Garde à vous!' The officers, their glasses abrim with purple wine, rise in unison. The young officer now announces, 'Attention à la poussière' ('Look out for the dust'). The glasses are drained and 'Boudin' is sung.

The legionnaires next fought in Italy. Austria had declared war on King Victor Emmanuel II of Sardinia and France supported him. This time there was no debate as to whether the Legion should participate, and both regiments were ordered from Algeria in 1859. The 1st Regiment (Colonel Chabrière) was by now all Swiss, but it was pathetically low in numbers—only 600 in all. With the 2nd Regiment, 1,500 men, it came under the command of General Éspinasse, formerly a Legion officer.

Their corps commander was Marshal MacMahon who well knew what legionnaires could do; as a colonel he had led two battalions of them against M'Chounech, the Kabyle stronghold in the Atlas Mountains, in 1844. Now he planned to use them as the spearhead of his attack on Magenta, 4th June 1859. They were paraded for his inspection, and MacMahon, standing in his stirrups, shouted to them, 'Legionnaires, tu es né pour mourir, et je 't'envoie là où on meurt'

('Legionnaires, you are born to die, so I am sending you where men get killed').

One of the first killed was Colonel Chabrière, shot storming the strong outpost of Marcollo; he was the third Legion commander to die at the head of his men. Major Martinez, an old Spanish guerrilla fighter and a great Legion character, assumed command, rallied his legionnaires and led them into the most vital part of the battle of Magenta, a fact often glossed over in French official army histories which give most of the credit to French regular battalions.

On 22nd June, near the small town of Solferino, the 2nd Regiment, now under the newly promoted Colonel Martinez, was acting as advance guard for the French 2nd Corps when it ran into the Austrian Army. Standing firm under withering fire, the regiment gave the French Corps time to come up into position. The battle was far-flung, fierce and bloody and Solferino was not cleared until the Legion took the enemy-held cemetery, one of the main positions dominating the defence.

An ordinary legionnaire killed in action was found, from his papers, to have been one of the seventeen Austrian generals who had been involved in a plot against Russia in 1849 and had been condemned to death. Ironically he died, in any case, at the hands of his own countrymen.

The sufferings of the soldiers at Solferino and the presence as an observer of the Swiss businessman, Henri Dunant, brought into existence the International Red Cross. The French victory brought acclaim to the 2nd Regiment Foreign Legion; the men were issued with new uniforms and they took part in a victory parade in Paris in August 1869.

Previously decorations had been scarce in the Legion; after Magenta and Solferino no fewer than thirty-five awards for bravery were issued. It was a brief hour of glory, but the best was yet to come.

In between these European wars the French prepared a thorough plan to occupy the Kabylia massifs, strongholds of their Moslem enemies. No fewer than fourteen expeditions had failed to gain a foothold in Kabylia, but now an army of thirty-five thousand was sent in, with the Legion as the advance guard of the column from the west. The way was blocked, in June 1857, by a large ridge on which was perched the well-defended village of Ischeriden. French regular regiments could not take it, but MacMahon, closely studying the hills through field glasses, found a small enemy camp higher up the ridge than the main position. He pointed this out to his Legion battalion commander and told him to take it and then advance downwards. Under heavy grape-shot the legionnaires scaled an escarpment and took the camp with the bayonet. Re-forming, they charged downhill onto the main enemy position and within half an hour held the entire ridge. They had not fired a shot.

The Arabs for long after this spoke in awe of the *grandes capotes*, referring to the great blue overcoats worn by the legionnaires. The display of discipline by the legionnaires was the talking point of the battle of Ischeriden, which soon led to the fall of all Kabylia. MacMahon himself inspected the legionnaires at Sidi Bel-Abbes and presented the 2nd Regiment with a new Colour with the honours 'Constantine 1837; Mostaganem 1839; Mouzaia 1840; Coleah 1841; Djidjelli 1842; Zaatcha 1849; Alma 1854; Sebastopol 1855'. Ischeriden was added later. It is fair to say that the presence of the *grandes capotes* was largely responsible for the success of the first and most difficult stage of the French conquest.

Chapter 8

The Greatest Glory

'Every legionnaire has "Camerone" engraved on his heart.' Legion maxim.

The French Foreign Legion wrote its most glorious page of history in Mexico. The French became interested in Mexico in 1862 and sent their client-ruler, the Austrian Archduke Maximilian, to the country in 1863. French troops had been in action as early as May 1862, and the Legion was at first disappointed and then incensed that it was apparently not wanted in the new arena. In a move that might have been regarded as mutiny in another force, the junior officers of the Legion, with the tacit approval of their seniors, collectively addressed a petition direct to the Emperor of France asking that the Legion be allowed to go and fight in Mexico.

They were not to know that the French Government had very nearly decided to *give* the Legion to Maximilian as it had given the earlier one to Spain. The ruse of having the petition signed only by the juniors did not deceive the French generals; they sacked the Legion colonel, Butet, and punished all the senior officers in one way or another—but the Legion was sent to Mexico. Its colonel was now Jeanningros, an efficient veteran of thirty years' service, including the battle of Moulay-Ishmael, Algeria. Two of his three battalions landed at Vera Cruz on 31st March 1863 and the third was preparing to follow.

The French, with forty thousand of their own troops and about thirteen thousand native auxiliaries, held Mexico City and Vera Cruz and a dangerous corridor between the two. The Mexican leader, Juarez, had twenty thousand troops in the north and a subordinate, General Diaz, had twenty thousand in the south. The Legion, to its bitter disappointment, found itself on escort and convoy duty in the eastern section, low, swampy land rife with hideous diseases such as yellow fever and typhus. This was soldiering without any frills and, apart from the incessant threat of guerrilla sniping, without real action.

64

At the end of April, four weeks after their arrival, the Legion was called on for a party to escort a bullion convoy to troops in the interior. The job fell to the Legion's 3rd Company, but all its officers were down with fever. Three other officers volunteered for duty—Captain Danjou the battalion adjutant, Lieutenant Vilain the pay officer and Second Lieutenant Maudet. They were a formidable trio. Danjou had been with the Legion for several years, serving with distinction in Algeria, Crimea and Italy. In the Crimea he had lost a hand and now wore a wooden one in its place. Vilain and Maudet were apparently French, though they had enlisted as other nationalities. They had come up through the ranks, had fought with efficiency and courage and had been commissioned because of their conduct at Magenta. They led a company of sixty-two *sous-officiers* and legionnaires, Polish, Italian, German and Spanish.

Mexican Intelligence was good, but even poor spies would have soon heard news of a bullion convoy. The local Mexican military leader, Colonel Milan, assembled two thousand troops—cavalry and infantry—to intercept and capture it. He anticipated no great difficulty, especially as his cavalry were efficient and armed with Remington and Winchester repeating rifles.

Early on 30th April the 3rd Company started well ahead of the bullion train to check that the route was clear, and at 2.30 a.m. called at a Legion defensive post along the corridor. Here the company commander was appalled at the smallness of the escort and offered Danjou a platoon as reinforcement. Danjou refused and moved on, with himself in the centre together with the ration and ammunition mules and the company in two wings, about 200 yards apart. Behind was a small rearguard section. Danjou had no scouts out, though as the Legion had no horsemen infantry scouts would have seen very little.

Just before 7 a.m. the 3rd Company passed through the deserted hamlet of Camaron, or Camerone as the French call it. It consisted of no more than a farmhouse and outbuildings enclosed in a courtyard and some derelict huts near by. A mile out of Camerone Danjou halted for breakfast and posted some sentries while water was boiled for coffee. It was the time of day legionnaires liked best.

Then came the alarm—enemy cavalry. Colonel Milan was approaching with eight hundred horsemen. Danjou's bugler sounded the call to arms and the legionnaires formed a square. They had only one natural advantage in that open country; scattered profusely were clumps of tropical vegetation and waist-high grass; something of a barrier for horsemen. Steady volleys from their Minie single-shot rifles kept the Mexicans back. Colonel Milan, not risking a charge, manœuvred his men to surround the Legion company. Danjou ordered a steady withdrawal to the only cover available—the farmhouse at Camerone. But the loss of his ration and ammunition mules which had galloped off in fright was a serious blow.

Now in smaller groups the Mexican cavalry circled the Legion company as it moved, hung tightly and harassed the men with sniping fire. Danjou warily moved his men through the thickest of the country to give the Mexicans no chance to charge. Twice he halted and fired a volley, which emptied some saddles.

But the horsemen had managed to cut off sixteen legionnaires, and when he reached the farmhouse Danjoy had only forty-six men, a few of them wounded. Even worse, he found that some Mexicans had reached the place before him and now held the upper floor and a barn in a corner of the courtyard.

It was an impossible position, but Danjou was a veteran legionnaire and accustomed to impossible situations. He ordered barricades across the openings and even managed to set up a perimeter defence against the walls and sheds, though much of the courtyard was exposed to fire from the Mexicans on the top floor and Danjou could do nothing to get at these men. The cavalry dismounted and tried several rushes, but the legionnaires beat them off. By 9 a.m. the sun was hot and Colonel Milan sent in an officer with a demand for surrender. Danjou refused, then went to each legionnaire and asked him to promise to fight until the end. His own end came at 11 a.m. when he was hit by a musket-ball fired by a sniper, probably from the barn.

Lieutenant Vilain took command and the defence was as steady as ever, but his thoughts when he saw the arrival of the Mexican infantry—1,200 men—can only be imagined. The firepower directed at the farmhouse was very heavy. The day became hotter and hotter and the legionnaires had no fluid other than in their water bottles and wine flasks.

Vilain's command was valiant until he too fell—a bullet hit him about 2 p.m. Second Lieutenant Maudet, himself handling a rifle, now rallied the survivors. Waves of attackers tried to swamp the defence, but the disciplined Legion fire stopped every one of them. From time to time a legionnaire would cross the bullet-swept courtyard to help a wounded comrade. The Mexicans set fire to straw near the courtyard walls and the afternoon became a stifling agony for Maudet's men. By 5 p.m. he counted twelve men who could stand on their feet, though some could only do so by leaning against the wall. He rejected several invitations to surrender—his replies, it is said, were in best barrack-room French—but then a massive

Mexican rush pushed him and his small band out of the farmhouse and into the only shelter left—a few outhouses. By 6 p.m. he had five men alive—Corporals Maine and Berg, Legionnaires Constantin, Leonard and Wensel. Collectively they had only a handful of ammunition. The approach of night could not help; it meant inevitable defeat. There are two versions of what happened next; it hardly matters which is the correct one, for both are incredible.

According to one account, Maudet ordered his men to fire their last rounds deliberately. Then, bayonets fixed, the group pulled aside a barricade and charged across the courtyard at the front ranks of 1,700 Mexicans. By the other account Maudet fell badly wounded and two of his men were killed as the tiny band withdrew from room to room until they could go no farther. Then, dazed, shocked and deafened they stood shoulder to shoulder against a wall, their bayonets held at guard. Certainly, Maudet was badly wounded and two men died. Corporals Maine and Berg and Legionnaire Wensel, a Pole, survived.

The Mexicans could hardly force themselves to kill these three men, but were about to go through the formality when a colonel, Chambas, sabre in hand, forced his way through and held back his men.

'Surely, you have to surrender now,' he said to the legionnaires.

Corporal Maine, glancing at his two comrades to check he was the senior survivor, said, 'We will surrender if you leave us our arms and permit us to tend our wounded.'

Chambas saluted him with his sabre. 'To a man like you I would grant anything.'

That's how the Legion's history relates the incident and it rings true, as does Colonel Milan's comment when told that only three legionnaires were on their feet. 'These are not men but demons.'

The Mexicans dragged twenty-three wounded legionnaires from the ruins and sixteen of them recovered. Maudet, being an officer, was given a slim chance to live. Put on a mule's back, he was taken to a hospital about fifty miles away and was carefully tended by the Spanish lady who conducted the hospital, but he had been too badly mauled and he died, as did a sergeant who was also taken to the hospital.

The Mexicans had killed 3 officers and 23 legionnaires; they lost 300 of their own troops killed and possibly as many as 500 wounded. And they did not capure the bullion. Danjou's forethought in having it follow at a safe distance paid off; hearing the firing the convoy halted until joined by Colonel Jeanningros and a relief force.

Jeanningros reached Camerone next day and took in the scene

with astonishment. He was even more astounded when his men discovered a single living legionnaire under the dead; this man had eight wounds and the Mexicans had left him for dead. He was able to give a coherent account of the action and is believed to have survived.

From a prison cell, Corporal Berg smuggled a note out to his colonel. It ended with the words, 'The 3rd Company is no more, but I must tell you it contained nothing but good soldiers.' Berg was commissioned on his return from captivity—the Camerone prisoners were exchanged on a one-for-one basis—and continued an already extraordinary career. He had been an officer in the French Regular Army and had fought in Algeria and Syria but was cashiered and joined the Legion as a private. Returning to Algeria after Mexican service he was killed in a duel with a fellow subaltern. Corporal Maine was also commissioned and became a captain. The other survivors were all honoured: Wensel, Schaffner, Fritz, Pinzinger and Brunswick were made Chevaliers of the Legion of Honour. Magnin, Palmaert, Kunassec, Schreiblick, Rebares and Groski received the Military Medal.

Even more important for Legion tradition, Captain Danjou's wooden hand was found in the ruins of Camerone and taken away to become the Legion's most prized possession—a sacred relic. Camerone Day became the Legion's ritual occasion, and it is celebrated with all the pomp and ceremony that the Legion can give it. Danjou's hand is paraded before the 1st Regiment at the base depot and the account of the battle is read to every Legion unit each Camerone Day. The ashes of the Camerone dead are preserved in a reliquary carved as the Mexican eagle and are held in rotation in the chapel of each Legion regiment. The Mexican eagle became the badge of the 1st Regiment.

Throughout their occupation of Mexico all French troops were ordered to halt when passing the farmhouse at Camerone and to present arms. The Mexicans were not so anxious to preserve the epic of Camerone and went to some trouble to reroute a railway line through the courtyard where so many of their men were killed. But they did leave part of the original wall, and in 1892 they permitted the French to erect a memorial with Latin and French inscriptions: 'Here there were less than sixty opposed to a whole army. Its mass crushed them. Life abandoned these French soldiers before courage. The 30th of April, 1863.' Later a bigger monument was erected, and in 1963 the French Army flew a large Legion contingent to Camerone for a centenary commemoration service.

For many years Camerone Day has been observed at Camerone,

attended by French residents in Mexico and by Mexican officers. Since 1904 it has been ceremonially observed in every Legion post, under fire if necessary.

The Mexican campaign also gave the Legion one of its worst defeats and worst memories and, ironically, it was psychologically the result of Camerone. Under Marshal Bazaine, the ex-Legion sergeant commanding all French forces in Mexico, the tradition and example of Camerone had taken root in the Legion and all legion-naires abhorred having to withdraw before the Mexicans. They were growing increasingly arrogant now because the United States was openly aiding Juarez. More than anything the Legion wanted to meet the Mexicans in a pitched battle, and to the 2nd Battalion, under Major Brian, such an opportunity seemed to come.

Brian was at Parras, northern Mexico, and was under orders to move south, and even stricter instructions not to venture into enemy-held territory without top-level authority. But he heard that a band of Mexicans was quartered at Santa Isabella, a farmhouse eight miles away. Desperate to avenge Camerone, Brian saw this as his great military opportunity, and in the early hours of 28th February 1866 he set off with 6 other officers and 188 legionnaires. Brian was walking straight into a baited trap, and within minutes of its being sprung Brian and eighty men were dead under volleys of bullets fired at close range, in the dark and from three directions. Captain Moulinier, infected by Brian's wish for vengeance, made one blind attack after another, but by 4 a.m.—after only three hours—every legionnaire had been killed, wounded or captured, except one. He escaped back to Parras to tell the story. The legionnaires taken by the Mexican infantry were slaughtered; only those captured by the better disciplined cavalry survived. The Legion had learned that it was not enough to have Camerone engraved on the heart; some discretion was necessary. Camerone did not mean disobedience of orders but strict obedience to them.

Neverthless during 1866 two successful engagements stand out among the many in which the Legion was involved. On 15th October the 1st Battalion took a large force of guerrillas by surprise and defeated them. In December about fifty mounted legionnaires—they were horsed for convenience and did not fight as cavalry—were surrounded at Perral. Their five hundred Mexican opponents made seven fruitless attempts to overrun the Legion detachment, which held out until relief arrived.

In February 1867 Bazaine, under orders from Paris, marched out of Mexico City at the head of his two divisions of French troops. Paris had decided that the Mexican adventure was over, and they

69

abandoned Maximilian to his fate. It was to be death by shooting, While he waited at Queretaro for his execution he wrote, 'I can only say that the Foreign Legion has been heroic.'

The Legion was not sorry to see the end of Mexico, but it left behind 31 officers and 1,917 legionnaires. There was nobody to mourn them and in all Mexico the only sign of the five years the French Army spent in Mexico is the monument at Camerone.

Apart from Camerone it returned to Sidi Bel-Abbes with other legends. The most intriguing concerns the capture of a small town by a French force, including a strong Legion detachment. The general in command, to show the shy inhabitants that the French were Christians like themselves, and not barbarians as they were represented to be, decided on a parade celebration of High Mass. To make the service as imposing as possible the troops decorated the church with palms and flowers, officers and men put on their full uniforms, and the drummers and buglers were placed so that they could beat and sound the salute at the elevation of the Host. But when all was ready no priest could be found—the *curé* of the parish had run away, and the monks of a neighbouring monastery refused to open their gate or to hold any communication with the conqueror. The general was on the point of renouncing the service and ordering the men to be marched away when the sentry on the church door presented arms as the general passed, and asked permission to speak to him.

'What do you want?' said the general.

'I was thinking, *mon général*, that if you cannot find a priest to perform the functions of the Mass I could do it just as well.'

'You! What do you mean?'

'I mean,' replied the legionnaire, 'that before I became a soldier I was a bishop, and that, never having been unfrocked, I am a priest still.'

The general consented to the man's performing the service. Putting on the vestments that were found in the vestry, and with the assistance of a lieutenant as an acolyte, the legionnaire performed the service of the Mass with perfect dignity, and the inhabitants were reassured as the general had hoped they would be. This ex-bishop was said to have been such a good fighter that he was decorated for exceptional bravery during the campaign.[33]

No real authentication of this story exists, but stranger things have been reported in the Legion and are known to be true.

Chapter 9

To Build an Empire

Algeria was rarely quiet and the tribes were especially violent while the French were at war with the Germans, 1870–1. Some Legion battalions were involved, but generally they had no more success than the other units of the French Army; the Germans hopelessly outclassed the French. The legionnaires' most bitter fighting was during the period of the Paris Commune—the civil war—which followed the war with Germany. For several weeks the legionnaires were engaged in street fighting, forcing one barricade after another. Several distinguished foreigners served as Legion officers for the duration only; one was the future King Peter of Serbia, a mere subaltern in the Legion.

With the war over, the French Army devoted itself to further North African pacification. More territory was needed, for under the harsh German peace terms France lost the province of Alsace and most of Lorraine, so many Frenchmen preferred to emigrate to Algeria rather than live under German rule. The French took large areas of fertile land from the rebellious tribes and gave it to the colonists, who stayed until thrown out after the French Algerian War of 1954–62.

When the supply of French colonists dried up the French gathered in Spaniards, Italians, Corsicans, Maltese and Sardinians. One group of Spaniards settled at Sidi Bel-Abbes; its women made a profession of marrying Legion *sous-officiers*. As traders and colonists arrived the legionnaires built a church, schools, a police station and administrative buildings; they planted rows of trees along the streets and engineered a water supply. Few of the 120,000 Algerians who inhabit the place today realize that they owe its existence to the Legion. The Algerians and Moroccans, indeed no North Africans, ever understood the legionnaires. They were Moslems, brought up

71

on the Koran, which teaches that the purpose of life is prayer and talk and reflection, not work and energy and productivity. They saw the legionnaires stripped to the waist, bareheaded, toiling at roads and bridges and tunnels and considered them fools and, by Koranic teaching, infidels. Many a sweating legionnaire, sourly eyeing the Berbers who squatted in the shade to look at him, would say to his comrade, 'What the hell are the bastards thinking?'

The Legion settled down to a fairly dull existence, more as a labour corps than a fighting force between 1871 and 1881 when Colonel Mallaret commanded them. In that year the Legion acquired its best CO to that time—the energetic, intelligent Colonel Négrier. If the hard-bitten legionnaires ever loved a CO it was Négrier. Among his many innovations was the formation of a type of mounted infantry, with two legionnaires to one mule. Each man took it in turn to ride the mule for an hour; in this way Legion columns covered more than thirty miles a day. Négrier, a thoughtful man, designed a special ammunition pouch worn high on the chest, where it could be got at more readily than from a leather case on the front of the belt, especially when a soldier was lying down behind cover.

Under Négrier, the seven-flamed grenade became the official Legion cap badge in 1882. Its first mention in Legion records is just before the Crimean War; the grenade itself, as an emblem, has always been the badge of any French *corps d'élite*, and the Legion so considered itself. Official recognition boosted their morale.

The Legion by now had its entrenched formalities and customs, official and unofficial, but all of which the *bleu* learnt the hard way. During his first few days the recruit would barter his cup of pinard for three cigarettes; he soon found out that by holding out long enough he could get ten cigarettes from the old sweats. Again, though volunteering for anything usually meant more work, it did pay to volunteer to fetch the sections' wine ration, for the man who fetched it had the right to distribute it and there was always half a litre over after each man had received his portion, or *quart*.

When a *sous-officier* entered the room the first man to see him had to shout 'Garde-à-vous!' and everybody came to attention. For an officer the shout was 'Fixe!' and off came the kepi. Presenting himself to an officer, the legionnaire opened the door smartly, marched smartly to a point six paces in front of the officer's desk, saluted, removed his kepi with his left hand. He then said, 'Legionnaire Brown. (So many years and months of service.) À vos ordres, mon capitaine.'

Away from base, adventure was never far off. In April 1882 a detachment of surveyors and cartographers was working along the

Moroccan border in the centre of territory occupied by the Ouled Sidi Cheikh tribesmen. Escorted by three hundred legionnaires, the party halted on the night of 25th April at a small well, near the desolate Chott Tigri valley. Next morning they moved into the valley and ran into a sandstorm, ideal cover for the 1,800 Arab horsemen and 6,000 other tribesmen who came yelling down from the hills. Surprised, the legionnaires formed three squares, and each fought a battle of its own. The mounted company was in the worst position on unfavourable ground, and Arab infiltrators prevented any junction with the main square.

When the two officers were killed a veteran legionnaire took command, and from behind a rampart of dead mules the men beat off several rushes. The enemy swarmed around the squares for seven hours, occasionally capturing a legionnaire to torture and mutiliate him before killing him. When the Arab mass drew off to regroup the Legion quickly formed one large square with the wounded inside and made a slow withdrawal, accurate rifle fire keeping off the Arab horsemen who harassed the flanks. As dusk fell Colonel Négrier arrived with a relief column, but two officers and forty legionnaires had been killed and three officers and twenty-eight men wounded. One officer survived with seven sword cuts and nine bullet wounds.

Somehow reports of incidents such as this reached the outside world, and without ever seeking it the Legion began to acquire an international reputation. It was at this period that retired legionnaires, men as well as officers, began to publish their reminiscences in their own countries, often embellishing facts which needed no embellishment. The novelists who got hold of the central theme misunderstood the facts, so that the Legion, a fighting force, became confused with the notorious Bataillons d'Afrique, the penal units in which military and civil criminals lived a brutish life.

The legionnaires feared capture more than death, for capture meant horrible tortures and mutilation, generally at the hands of the Arab women. Legion reprisals, though much less frequent, could be as severe as those of the Arabs. In some dissident villages one man in three was shot and there was a half hour of mass rape before the village was burned.

The French were unlucky about Africa. The British, Spanish, Dutch and Portuguese had already taken the more desirable prizes, and the best France could do, other than in Algeria, was to establish small posts along the coasts. Three of these were in Dahomey, a native African kingdom between what are now Ghana and Nigeria. The Dahomian troops frequently raided and looted the French settlements; they also sold captured natives into slavery and

73

sacrificed others. In August 1892 the able mulatto general, Dodds, led four thousand French troops—about half of them legionnaires —to take Dahomey by force and capture King Behazin.

Dahomey was a country of jungle, tropical forest, swamp and rivers. It was rife with tropical disease, especially malaria, and its people were bloodthirsty. The King of Dahomey had an annual bloodbath, and on this great holiday of the Dahomey year about five hundred people were beheaded for his pleasure. The Dahomey system of warfare against the other native races was notably successful, the troops marching in complete silence during the night along little-known routes to surround a town or village. The surprise attack at dawn was invariably successful. The best captives were carried off to the slave dealers and the others were ceremonially killed.

When the Legion was marching to meet it the Dahomey army had 10,000 male warriors and a corps of 1,500 women soldiers, courageous, able and ferocious. The whole army had been given some form of training by European soldiers-of-fortune and adventurers and many had modern firearms—the proceeds from slave bartering.

The Amazon army of Dahomey had seen its best days. Under King Gezo, who reigned until 1858, they were the best disciplined, best trained and most formidable fighting force in West Africa. But even now they were the *élite* formation of the army. They were divided into companies of about three hundred and were led by women officers, who wore a white head-dress to denote rank. Usually the 'uniform' was full skirt and a blouse, with a cartridge belt slung over shoulder or worn at the waist; a haversack and water gourd hung at their side and from their belts dangled bones taken from their victims. Naturally tough—African women customarily do the hard work while the men laze about—the Amazons had been brought up to carry heavy loads on their heads and think nothing of it. The best of the Dahomey women, picked for their physique and trained to march long distances, could outfight any men. Those of the king's bodyguard had precedence in the army, while all others had equal standing with the male soldiers. Some foreign visitors to Dahomey said that the Amazons were celibate and strictly kept apart from the male units. Nothing pleased a Dahomey king more than to show off his female warriors, especially in a charge over a demonstration battle course where the main obstacles were thorn barriers.

The Legion had heard about the Amazons, but the men were not too perturbed about them. There was no point in killing them, many of the men said, when they could easily be disarmed and raped. After the brothels of Algeria it would be interesting to have sex with real women, whom the legionnaires pictured in their minds as ravishingly beautiful.

Just how beautiful these women were it is now difficult to say. To a sex-starved legionnaire almost any woman had allure, but pictures of the time showed Dahomey Amazons with round, shaved heads, lank legs and pointed teeth. André Gide said that these girls, erect in the bright light, shining with oil or dripping with river water, were like a fruit of a tree or a ferocious animal. He explained that what moved him and others was the strangeness of their beauty and their absence of mock-modesty.

They also had no fear and led most of the daily attacks made on the marching column. Nevertheless the Legion's first action, at Dogba on 18th September 1892, was successful. Caught at dawn in a pincer movement and under such pressure that their square was broken, the legionnaires held firm and left 825 dead enemy. They were vastly impressed by the Amazons as soldiers. Some legionnaires, being chivalrous to a wounded woman soldier, were shot or speared. These women asked for no quarter and gave none.

At one time, at Cana, General Dodds made a speech to the Legion, saying he considered them to be the finest soldiers in the world and was extremely proud of having had the privilege of commanding them. 'We swallowed this incontrovertible fact,' wrote Legionnaire Frederic Martin, 'just as if it had been the rankest flattery.' [34]

Dodds's command of the expedition was superlative. The column had to be supplied, and the ration parties, carrying loads on their heads, provided the shuttle service between it and the coast, bringing up ammunition and provisions. They had to be heavily escorted and many were ambushed or had their halting camps raided. That Dodds could continue his advance despite his dwindling numbers was a tribute to his persistence, but, as he said later, only the Legion could have done what was needed. Dodds reached Abomey on 6th November, just after the king had fired his capital and evacuated it. The legionnaires who took possession were intrigued by the 'cobbled floors' they were walking on, until they realized that the cobbles were the skulls of the victims of sacrifice embedded in the earthen floors— tens of thousands of them. Many of the drinking vessels were parts of human skulls. Behazin was captured two days later and exiled.

The Legion marched back to the coast; 450 men were fit enough to walk onto the troopship. Not one of them could truthfully boast that he had raped an Amazon, but the force of women warriors rapidly broke up under French rule.

Many legionnaires died in the service of France without the least idea of what France was trying to accomplish with their blood and sweat. One dream of French statesmen was a transcontinental railway crossing Africa from the Mediterranean to the Ivory Coast, via Timbuktu. The railway crept slowly southwards, but the vast hinterland had to be 'pacified', which meant killing or capturing many notorious slave-dealers, particularly Sultan Ahmadu and 'Samory', a ruthless Senegalese.

Colonel Archinand had the unenviable task of chasing these powerful, cunning men, but he found the native troops allotted to him too weak in spirit. Aware that ordinary French troops could neither stand the pace nor the rigours of the vast areas they would have to cover, he asked for legionnaires. The Legion at Sidi Bel-Abbes and Saida called for volunteers, specifying that they must be under twenty-five and the toughest of the tough. How many legionnaires so regarded themselves is not recorded, but in September 1892 a company of 120 men arrived at Kayes, Guinea. They were organized as mounted infantry, a mule to each man. Nobody had mentioned riding as a qualification, but the legionnaires quickly learned how to handle their mules.

In two groups the legionnaires accompanied columns of native troops, and though they could stand the physical strain of their mission they were often distressed by the destruction and death left by the slave-raiders. These ruthless men burnt prosperous villages and their crops, leaving only a few people alive, those so old they would not have brought a sou on the market. Occasionally the legionnaires found alive a baby hidden by its mother and overlooked by the raiders. The slave bands were hard to track and even more difficult to bring to a fight, but the legionnaires gave no quarter when they managed it.

These Legion soldiers travelled as far as most soldiers in history and farther than most. They operated in Upper Guinea, Senegal, Upper Volta, the Sudan and parts of Nigeria. They reached as far as Karo, on the Sassandra River, in deepest Sudan. The bald statement in Legion records that in a little over a year they marched twelve thousand miles, crossed twelve major rivers and fought fourteen major engagements conceals great courage and endurance. Just why they were returned to Algeria when they had been so successful is not known. Present-day Legion officers shrug and put it down to the jealousy of Regular French Army officers who could not get their men to do half as much.

But surveying and exploration and pacification went on from other bases, often with the Legion acting on its own. They became explorers on some of their expeditions, as on the march, April–July 1900, from Gerryville across the Sahara to the oases of Timimoun;

then they circled along the southern foothills of the Great Atlas as far as Afloa before returning to Gerryville. The legionnaires covered 1,200 miles in seventy-two days, through unmapped country, without knowledge of wells or water-holes, running the constant risk of being attacked by savage, hostile tribes. It was a superb performance, and although it achieved no element of pacification, fighting was continual at fort and in mountain pass, at oasis or native village.

Yet the great majority of legionnaires wore no socks when route-marching because they chafed the feet. Some of the men wrapped their feet in a triangular piece of linen which they called a *chaussette russe*. But in most cases nothing was worn inside the boot. Legionnaire George Manington found this comfortable over a long distance, but the boots had to fit well at the heel, ankle and instep, so that the foot did not slip. 'They should be broad across the toes, and about half an inch longer than the foot itself; and, most important of all, should be so well greased that the leather of the uppers is as supple as india-rubber.'[35] Legionnaires suffered from blistered feet as a simple fact of life. The Legion method of curing blisters was to pass a greased thread through them, snipping the ends off each side to let them drain and smearing the whole inflamed part with tallow.

It seemed to the French Government that the subjugation of North-West Africa was taking too long, and a serious study was made to find a man able enough to see all the problems at once and to master them. They sent Colonel Louis Hubert Lyautey, aged forty-nine. This energetic, intelligent and diligent officer was above all a man of system. He looked at his overloaded troops—regulars as well as legionnaires—and stripped them of heavy equipment and baggage. The idea was not to be humane but to enable the men to march farther and faster. Lyautey also evolved a complex plan of patrolling; various units met at key points and operated much as single guards do around an armed camp. He pushed the rebels out of the great Figuig district, then cleared the region to the Moroccan border. Setting up Colomb Béchar, Forthassa and Berguent as bases, Lyautey sent out his fighting patrols. In three years he had driven most of his enemies into Morocco.

This was progress, but the Algerian tribes occasionally raided from Morocco, so the French, by some protracted political manœuvres, obtained 'permission' from the Great Powers to occupy Morocco and waited for an excuse to do so. It came with the murder of a French doctor, and the Legion, with other troops, moved into Oujda in March 1907. By the end of September the Legion had taken part in several actions and one thousand of the legionnaires were concentrated for the first major test of strength—the attack on the fortress of Mediouna, fifteen miles from Casablanca. The French commander, General Drude, had only two thousand men in all. The coolness of the legionnaires under fire and their disciplined precision—when moving in square they halted to fire and then moved on—were in stark contrast to the ragged lines of the ordinary French units.

War correspondents with the French Army, at first inclined to ignore these 'mercenaries', were even more impressed than General Drude. It was their agitation which induced the Government to pay the Legion the extra active service bonus until now denied them.

The Legion in square was an impressive sight. Calmly, with bayonets fixed, they marched through villages at their steady, relentless pace, hardly pausing when it came to a kill, passing prisoners back with a hefty kick. On the open plain they knelt to fire at charging cavalry.

Yet for all the skill and courage shown by the legionnaires France was a long time subduing Morocco. They did not capture Fez until June 1911, but this gave them a corridor to the coast, and as usual the Legion built blockhouses to protect this corridor and then manned them. Reconnaissance was always dangerous. At Ksar d'Alouna thirty-five legionnaires were sent to check the village, and while passing through a shallow basin near it were ambushed. Pinned down, the legionnaires kept back much greater numbers of Arabs for five hours until two strong companies arrived. By then only six legionnaires were alive. A corporal had had the presence of mind to hide in his uniform the bolts of the rifles of his dead comrades so that they could not be used by the enemy; then he too had been killed.

Steadily the French worked at linking routes between Algeria and Morocco, but this took until 1914, with heavy fighting all the way. A principal Legion action occurred on 4th June when the Legion scrambled up craggy hillsides to force back Moroccans massed there. After this action the *sous-officiers* and the legionnaires of the Legion battalion wrote to General Lyautey asking that their commander, Major Met, be promoted for his leadership and courage. Met became a lieutenant-colonel; perhaps the unconventional recommendation helped. He lost a leg fighting the Germans on the French Western Front a few months later. The Great War reduced the operations in North Africa to 'holding actions'.

Chapter 10

'Minor' Campaigns

'Men who have nothing to lose no more need courage to confront danger than a man who has lost all hope needs courage to commit suicide.' Colin John, quoting Sergeant Manual Lopez y Garcia in Indo-China.

The French Army had been active in Indo-China for about thirty years before the Legion managed to find its way there, at the 'invitation' of Colonel Négrier, in 1883. As Colonel of the Regiment, Négrier had come to like the legionnaires as they liked him, and when he was posted to Indo-China—or Tonkin as the French called it—he induced Army HQ to include Legion units.

Despite the unfamiliar terrain and jungle vegetation the legionnaires quickly adapted themselves to new tactics; they were successful in their first action on 16th December, the capture of the fort of Son-Tay, held by the 'Black Flags', the Chinese troops trying to spread south through Indo-China. Nothing is known of Legionnaire Minaert except his name and the fame he won at Son-Tay. He was the first to climb the wall of the citadel. Despite the heavy load he carried he climbed the wall like a cat and, fighting off the enemy, secured the ladder up which his comrades swarmed. The exploit is depicted in the Legion museum's hall of memory.

The Legion fought one of its greatest battles in Indo-China when 20,000 Chinese surrounded the fort of Tuyen-Quang, held by 390 French, half of them legionnaires. It was a position the veteran legionnaires knew only too well. The fort was brick-built and square, with a double line of walls. The Chinese first attacked on 26th January 1885, and made several attacks by tunnelling and mining. One explosion blew a few legionnaires over the parapet into the path of onrushing Chinese, and without orders comrades rushed out to rescue them. Some Chinese mines created great breaches, but in savage bayonet fighting the legionnaires held the enemy. The Legion officers believed that an audacious raid would break Chinese morale, so a detachment, in a night foray, cleared an enemy trench and so confused the enemy that they lost two of their standards. The impudent sortie reacted the wrong way, for the Chinese made several spirited attacks, but on the night of 2nd March, with a Legion relief column approaching, they did pull out.

Actions of this sort, raids against Chinese positions, ambushes, hard marching through jungle trails against elusive guerrillas and bandit gangs led by war-lords, continued until 1895, when the last action in this phase of the conquest of Indo-China took place. The Legion settled down for a long spell of garrison duty in far more congenial surroundings—among the Congais—than their comrades in Algeria.

That same year, with Indo-China temporarily quiet, the French politicians—opportunists as empire-builders—saw the great island of Madagascar as potential territory and sent an expedition which included a Legion *bataillon de marche*. Unaware of the mountainous nature of much of the terrain, the difficulties of climate and the fighting potential of the native warriors, the Hovas, the Government gave General Duchesme only a small force. It is reported that when he asked for a stronger army the reply was, 'Well, you have a Legion *bataillon de marche*.' This was comforting, but Duchesme soon found that the Hovas had been trained by British and other European officers, and that some were armed with Remington and Schneider rifles, Hotchkiss machine-guns and a few light artillery pieces.

The Hovas adopted a scorched earth policy, but they would rarely stand long against the fierce assaults of the 'Lambas Blancs', as they called the legionnaires. Tramping in full marching order through difficult jungle country, infested with malarial mosquitoes and other insects, was tough campaigning. Rations were on half supply and medical supplies short. The Legion suffered, but because of discipline, and their tendency not to mix with the other French troops, they lost fewer men. With fever taking heavy toll among the regular units the Legion spent most of its time, when it was not road-building, at the head of the column.

Through May, June, July, August, September they cut their way through thick jungle. By 10th September, when reinforcements arrived from Algeria, the original Legion force was down to 19 officers and 450 men. This group formed the spearhead of 4,000 men Duchesme proposed to use on a 'lightning' march on Tananarive, the capital. This was 125 miles away, so everybody knew it was desperate effort. The legionnaires called it the *marche ou crève* column; this means literally 'march or croak'. As 'March or Die' the phrase became a basic part of Legion language and philosophy.

The task force moved off on 15th September, and on 28th September sighted the queen's palace, which dominated the city of Tananarive. The city fell after a mere fifteen minutes' fighting, and a few days later a Legion detachment was installed as guard at the palace. It did not seem so much of an honour for the 226 dead legionnaires left along the jungle trails, all but five dying from illness.

Legionnaires have never been left in one place for long, and by December the survivors were back in Algeria—unhappily so, for they found the Madagascan women desirable and obliging. Legion absence from Tananarive was brief. In March 1896 rebellion broke out and threatened to be more dangerous than the original war. General Gallieni, now in command, asked Legion HQ in Sidi Bel-Abbes for six hundred young legionnaires who had seen jungle service in Indo-China. He used these men in strong patrols to penetrate the mountain and jungle fastnesses to keep the rebels on the run and, gradually, to 'pacify' them. But this was a hard task and other Legion units were needed. Pacification was not complete until 1901, and even then Legion units were frequently used to awe the Hova tribesmen. The French administration did not feel safe without Legion units until 1905, by which time many legionnaires were reluctant to leave. As usual they left behind them roads, bridges, docks and public buildings.

Wherever the legionnaire was sent he could always count on being returned to North Africa, usually first to Sidi Bel-Abbes and then to garrisons in Tunisia, Algeria or Morocco. The Legion was always marching somewhere, so that a stranger might have thought it must be a very large force; in fact it never exceeded thirty-five thousand in North Africa and was generally smaller, about eight thousand in 1912. Similarly the inhabitants must have believed that the Legion was omnipresent, an effect achieved by the use of hundreds of patrols. Erwin Carlé, the German who served in the Legion early in the century, has given a graphic description of what marching meant to the individual legionnaires: 'It is always drummed into the legionnaire that he is intended for nothing else in this world except marching. If the pangs of hunger are gnawing at his stomach or thirst parches his tongue, that is so much the worse for him, but is no sort of reason for not marching on! He may be tired, dead tired, completely exhausted—but he must not stop marching. If his feet are bleeding and the soles burn like fire, that is very sad—but marching pace must not be slackened. The sun may burn until his senses are all awhirl, he must go on. His task in life is to march. The greatest crime he can commit is to fail on the march. There is no such thing as an impossible marching assignment for the regiment of foreigners.

Each individual is inoculated with the one idea, it is hammered into him, that he has to march as long as he can control his legs. And when he can no longer control them, then he must at least try to crawl.' [36]

Officers no less than men felt the despair and mental dehydration produced by the unending monotony of the desert. Lieutenant Cortier, who crossed the Tanezruft in 1905, was at first delighted. 'My first encounter filled me with wonderment. Here at last was a place where one could think, gather one's thoughts, analyse them, where indeed one had nothing else to do but look inward.' Gradually depression settled on him: 'Once again the day's route unrolled itself before you, sad, immensely sad, on the eternal lustreless ground and under the grey sky. The hours lengthened and dragged on desperately slowly while the mind wandered off, reliving old memories, thinking over and over again thoughts already mulled a thousand times, clutching at all memories of the past and all the hopes of the future. Little by little, the emptiness of earth and sky created an emptiness in the mind as one went on through this dreadful solitude, broken, heavy of heart and with unseeing eyes.' [37]

Throughout all their trials and temptations the legionnaires nursed their secrets, but once in a while—as with the legionnaire-bishop in Mexico—something would happen to give a glimpse into a man's past. In Tunisia a legionnaire was drowned at Zarzis while trying to save a fisherman whose boat had capsized. The dead man's comrades made a coffin out of packing-cases, the boards retaining the original inscriptions, one of which was 'Keep the Contents Dry'. No priest was available, but an Italian legionnaire stepped out of the ranks and, announcing that he was a priest, recited the committal service from memory, which was perhaps a pretty fair proof of his original calling.[38]

As European tensions and enmities developed in the years before 1914 the German Foreign Office mounted a violent campaign against the Legion, protesting that no modern state had any right to call foreign subjects to its defence. In a vehement document, the Germans listed all the vices and shortcomings of the Legion—drunkenness, homosexuality and immorality of every kind. Recruiting sergeants, the Germans said, got young men drunk, made them false promises and signed them up. As usual the French—and the Legion—ignored the German protest. The German action was designed not merely to defame the French and their Legion but to retrieve from it experienced German soldiers who would be useful in training a German army for European conflict. At this time the Legion desertion rate was high, so perhaps the German propaganda had some effect.

In counterbalance, most men who deserted did so during their first year of service.

Also many legionnaires were enlisting for a second and even a third period of five years. North Africa has a magic which affects even insensitive men, and many legionnaires were acutely sensitive. They were awed by the dry, harsh heat and they were enchanted by the cool shadows and the glistening waters. Night in the Arab towns was not merely a cover for visits to bordellos and hashish-sellers; it was a doorway into another world with smells and sights and sounds unknown to these men from other countries. The alleys, the souks (bazaars), casbahs (the word really means fortress) and medinas (markets) and the whole poetry of North Africa kept men in the Legion as much as any other influence.

In truth, the Legion was not such a bad life for a man who could stay out of trouble. Frederic Martin and a Russian comrade, Petrovski, made the discovery that *sous-officiers* could be tipped. It had to be done delicately, usually by asking the sergeant to accept a present or by leaving a present where he could find it. 'A packet of cigarettes or of tobacco, a bundle of cigars, or a bottle of sealed wine, will never offend a sergeant or a corporal if given by a good soldier who is not likely to expect anything more than goodwill in return, but the goodwill of a non-commissioned officer is very useful sometimes, and his ill-will is a misfortune always.'[39] Martin emphasized that it was not necessary to bribe non-coms to get them to behave decently towards a legionnaire. It was generally those *sous-officiers* who were most popular by reason of their fairness who received these 'little attentions'.

By 1914 legionnaires were conscious of being different from other soldiers. The famous kepi blanc—the white cap—helped greatly in this, although pith helmets and other head covering were worn in various campaigns. Nobody knows the origin of the kepi blanc. It just happened, and the Legion adopted it as official head-dress long after most men were wearing it. It seems to have appeared first in 1840 when a white cover, with an attached neckcloth, was worn as protection against the sun. In the 1880s a khaki cap cover was issued, but with constant washing and the sun it bleached almost white. Recruits, issued with a deep khaki-coloured cover, hastily scrubbed it until it faded, in the hope that they would be taken for old campaigners. From that time the off-white kepi blanc was worn by all legionnaires in Algeria. The true kepi blanc was issued in 1939 and was worn on parade for the first time in Paris. In 1914 the legionnaires, like most of the soldiers of Europe, would soon be wearing steel helmets. And they would need the psychological

83

strength which comes from being members of an élite, though it should be noted that neither the Legion as a body nor individual legionnaires were particularly offended when the corps was not given full credit for their share in a battle or campaign. They merely wanted to be recognized as formidable, tough—and different. This difference was about to be put to its greatest test.

Chapter 11

The Furnace of World War I

'Who cares that the dogs bark when the Legion passes?' Colonel Rollet, Commandant of the Legion in France 1917–18 and 'Father of the Foreign Legion'.

A conventional account of the French Foreign Legion in World War I might begin with dates and places and battles. But a much better picture of the colourful and hybrid nature of the Legion at this period in its history is given in a letter written to his mother by an English recruit in the Legion in the first months of 1914. He was J. Woodall Marshall. 'I have been in many places and have had strange experiences, but never in all my life have I struck anything so wonderfully romantic and extraordinary as the French Foreign Legion. I am, after three days' experience as a recruit, not at all put out by the actuality. The Legion is the strangest thing ever thought of by the mind of man. In my room, which is comfortable, there is myself, an Irishman, an American, and the other inhabitants include an ex-officer in the army of the So. American Republic, who came specially over from South America for the war, and is my greatest friend, a Dutch solicitor, a Russian Jew, three Cossacks, two Italians, a student from a Russian University, an Englishman who has always been resident in Paris and who can hardly speak English, a Spaniard, and other mysterious individuals whose identity is absolutely hid.

'I have only signed on for the duration of the war, probably six months, but of course there are many old Legionaries [sic] who have been years in the Regiment, notably an Englishman, who has been seventeen years in the Legion, a gentleman and a thoroughly decent fellow. Of course these old hands are all disapppointed men, who have joined the Legion through all sorts of reasons—scandal, disappointments in love, and anything that might drive a man to despair. Also there are the adventurers to whom the Legion has appealed through its romantic conditions. And the wonderful thing is that all these strange men coming from all over the world have knit themselves so much together that they are as one great family. Everyone is "my comrade", "my good friend". These words enter into every phrase. "Let me have a light, my good comrade," "Have a cigarette, my friend." It is wonderful, this life in the Legion.

'I have told you of the inhabitants of my room. The Legion includes men of every rank, rich and poor, but all under the same flag, "for honour", and all, as I have said, of one great family. We have counts and Jewish pedlars, millionaires and paupers, officers from foreign armies and deserters from all countries. I should not be a bit surprised if we could supply a bishop. If the electric light goes wrong an electrician comes forward. If a man hurts himself in exercise there is not any need to send for the regimental doctor. You can always for a sou get a tailor to mend your clothes or an ex-barber to give you a shave; an ex-cigarette maker will show you how to make a cigarette, and an old clothes merchant will tell you the exact value of your civilian clothes. But if I were to attempt to describe all the professions and occupations of the various legionaries I would exceed the amount of paper at my disposal and should probably be late for barracks tonight.

'I may, just as a sample of nationalities, give you a dozen or so out of the way people who are represented in the Legion. A Persian, a Japanese, a small bevy of Cossacks, a representative of every South American Republic, a full-blooded negro, a few dozen half-blooded worthies of every mixture imaginable. Montenegrins and the Balkan races generally and, well, almost every race under the sun, even an Esquimo. And the wonderful thing is that all these races have so taken upon themselves the doctrines of the Legion that everything runs as smoothly and as calmly as a first class hotel. It is a standing rule that no one shall put anyone else to any extra trouble and no one shall interfere with anyone else's business. Thus if a man were to take a bayonet and announce his intention of running himself through no one would interfere with him or advise him not to. But the orderly of his room would probably ask him, in the nicest manner possible, as a good comrade, not to do it in the room, as it would make a mess which he would have to clear up. Nobody thinks of asking anybody else his private life or the why or wherefore of his entry into the Legion. There is a complete absence of swearing. A complete calm, every idea is to save anybody else trouble. Everything is shared in common.

'On second thoughts I should almost liken the Legion to an extremely strict but well conducted monastery, except, of course, the complete absence of any religious exercises, though, mentioning the different religions, they are not wanting—Catholics, Protestants,

Jews, Mohammedans, members of the Russian Orthodox Church, and heaven knows what else. What the fighting qualities of the Legion, in a war like this, are, is a matter of conjecture, but I could not have greater confidence in the bravery and self-sacrifice of my comrades if I were in the finest crack corps any country could possess. I think I have dwelt enough on the peculiar qualities of my regiment, and you will, I think, understand that some of them might not shine in a drawing room, though, as to the latter some of them would shine uncommonly well. As a whole, they are quite capable of sending representatives to either a palace or a workhouse, and those representatives would not feel the slightest bit out of place.

'We cater for a very decent music hall display, possessing as we do, Vitas, "the strongest man in the world", who, by the way, has a rival in the Legion itself, a conjuror and a Japanese juggler. The American representative could give a very good ragtime exhibition, while I have no doubt the Cossacks would oblige with an example of rough riding. As for the sentimental and comic songs, well, there would be an embarrassment of riches.

'Our uniform is that of the ordinary French soldier—a blue tunic, overcoat turned over from the knees, a red képi, red trousers, with the exception of the distinctive addition of a blue sash which every Legionary wears, and is the only soldier in the French Army so habited. As for the life, it is not hard for me. I have always walked a good deal for pleasure, and marching is the great speciality of the Legion and I do not find it beyond me, though many I dare say would find it hard. To sum up, life is a strenuous but quite happy one ...'[40]

Marshall was serving in one of the several Legion *régiments de marche*, affiliated with the parent regiment. None of these legionnaires, enlisting for the duration, ever saw Sidi Bel-Abbes and North Africa. Many foreigners wanted to fight for France, but French law precluded their enlistment in the Regular Army; in the Legion they swore allegiance to the Legion flag, not to France, although training cadres of Legion officers and *sous-officiers* were sent from North Africa to train them at camps in Lyons, Avignon, Rouen and Toulouse.

Not all these recruits were as happy as Marshall. The Cossacks he referred to, twelve of them, could speak neither French nor Russian, and nobody knew from whence they came. They became morose and refused to eat. With some trouble an interpreter was found and he reported that the Cossacks had left home to join the French Foreign Legion Cavalry. But the Legion had no cavalry and these men, who had spent their lives in the saddle, found themselves expected to fight on foot and carry heavy loads. They were released.

There were even more ticklish problems than Cossack volunteers. The Legion had many German members and a few hundred, suspected of being more pro-Teutonic than pro-Legion, were interned in North Africa. The greater number of legionnaires from enemy countries were happy to stay in Morocco and serve the Legion. The French, with enough on their hands in Europe, wanted to do no more than remain static in North Africa. Legion forts beat off hundreds of attacks, but no punitive campaigns were mounted; they would require more men than the French could spare. Throughout the war Austrian and German volunteers came in steadily—men who preferred a fighting chance in the Legion to virtually no chance on the Western and Eastern fronts in Europe. Some German and Austrian legionnaires fought in Europe against their own people, knowing they would be executed if captured and identified.

Marshall had witnessed a change in the character of the Legion, largely because hundreds of young Americans eager to fight but unable to join any foreign army without endangering their citizenship could safely enlist in the Legion. The 1st Regiment was so Americanized that it became something of a tourist attraction and was probably visited by more French generals than any other unit on the front.

Not everybody was fascinated by the Legion in France, Americans or not. In some places, as they marched through towns, the mixture of strange languages convinced the local French that they were German prisoners, and they came under a barrage of stones, rotten eggs and bad fruit. Also, as Legion trains travelled north from the Mediterranean ports, the trains stopped at certain stations for the soldiers to buy food. The station-masters were instructed to shout 'Voici la Légion!' Many of them also added 'Fermez les portes!' In the face of such anti-Legion behaviour, to which the old hands were accustomed, the Americans learned how to fend for themselves —the old system of *démerdez-vous*. With all doors closed against them they lived well enough on their thefts.

These Americans were mostly young idealists, many of them students or former students of famous universities, while a few were typical Legion hard cases. Probably the best known of them was Alan Seeger, aged twenty-six when the war began. A handsome man, he was becoming established as a poet in Paris. The London *Daily Telegraph*, reviewing his collection of poems, had said, 'He belongs by birthright to the company of immortals.' He seemed also to belong to the company of men who fight for principles. 'I never took arms out of hatred against Germany or the Germans,' he wrote (31st July 1915), 'but purely out of love for France.'[41]

Seeger had an interesting experience when legionnaires held the château of Craonelle. A German shell blew open the sealed door of the Craonelle library, one of the greatest in France. With a fellow Harvard legionnaire, he gently handled priceless books and manuscripts. It was some recompense for day-to-day living in the family burial vaults, which formed the parados of the trenches.

Even war seemed poetic. Seeger wrote to his godmother on 4th June 1916, 'I have a presentiment that we are going into action. The last rumour is that we go to Verdun to relieve the 2nd Moroccan Division. That would be magnificent, wouldn't it? The long journey drawing nearer and nearer to that furnace, the distant cannonade, the approach ... full of dramatic scenes, the salutations of troops that have already fought, "Bon courage, les gars!" and then our own debut in some dashing affair.' Towards the end of the month he concluded another letter: 'I am glad to be going in the first wave. If you are in this thing at all it is best to be in to the limit. And this is the supreme experience.' With many fellow legionnaires he was killed during a charge at Belloy-en-Santerre, 4th July 1916.

One legionnaire, Charles Sweeney, having come to the Legion from West Point, worked his way up to a commission, but this did not result in lighter duties for his fellow Americans as they ruefully found out. Sweeney was later wounded in the head, but won American decorations and the French Croix de Guerre.

Some Americans were so wealthy they could afford anything they wanted, and when they spent their money they did so ostentatiously. Charles Drossner, member of a wealthy San Francisco family, regarded his first Legion meal sourly and said to the German sergeant, 'Do you expect me to eat that?'

'You didn't join the Legion to fill your belly,' his sergeant said. 'I am eating it too.'

'Yep, we're all in the same boat,' Drossner said as he took from his wallet three 1,000-franc notes. 'Let's hire the best chef in town.' Which they did.

One of the few professional American soldiers in the Legion was Edward Morlae of California; as a *sous-officier* it was his duty to coax, cajole and coerce this odd assortment of American individualists into a *team*. The German and French *sous-officiers* were glad to have Morlae around for they could do nothing with the Americans. They were said to be the dirtiest and most undisciplined of legionnaires, but they marched without complaint and always did well in rifle practice. The criticisms were unfair generalizations. The Americans fell into Legion ways, even to flavouring their French cigarettes with rum. Most of them even went sockless, Legion fashion. The professional *sous-officier*, Morlae, having won the Croix de Guerre, asked for leave, went to Spain and from there deserted back to the States where, as a Legion hero, he wrote articles for *Atlantic Monthly*. These highly coloured, vainglorious features infuriated the Americans still serving in the trenches.

American casualties were great, and after lamentably heavy losses in August 1915, and the discovery that several men who had enlisted as Belgians were German spies, there was a plan to break up the Legion. Many Americans then formed the Lafayette Escadrille of the French Air Force. Even fliers who entered aviation direct had first to enrol in the Legion, a technical device to circumvent the American Constitution. Those Americans still in the Legion saw deeds of incredible valour and frightful carnage. In one attack in Champagne two battalions of the Legion and one of the Chasseurs Alpins were caught on the German barbed wire and died to a man, in rows.

When the United States officially entered the war virtually all Americans in the Legion were automatically transferred to the American forces, but it was now legally possible for them to transfer to the French Army. Commandant Rosé, the very gallant leader of the 2nd Legion Regiment, called the transferees together. 'You are leaving the Legion,' he said. 'For God's sake don't spread the usual lies about it. We are not all perverts, cut-throats and sneak thieves. We are men who have had troubles of our own. We are a hard-fighting regiment of professional soldiers and we have won a glorious name. Don't go and smirch it.'

Other nationalities had already gone. In March 1915 the Legion released large numbers of foreign volunteers, mainly those who had joined it before their own countries had entered the war; batches of Russians, Belgians and Italians were discharged, and one small group of British including Woodall Marshall, who, as a lieutenant with the Northumberland Fusiliers, won the Military Cross but was killed in action.

One *régiment de marche* was largely Italian and included five members of the Garibaldi family, which gave it the nickname of the 'Garibaldi brigade'. This unit was in action in the Argonne in December 1914 and, caught by German machine-guns as they crossed a ravine, they lost 4 officers and 44 men killed and another 170 wounded. Two days later they took some trenches at bayonet point but lost 125 killed and 172 wounded. Two members of the Garibaldi family died. The brigade lost 429 killed before Italy entered the war and the survivors were released to join their national army.

The Legion battalions suffered no less severely than the French and British regular battalions. In May 1915, during the battle of Artois the Legion took 3,000 yards of territory at a cost of 2,200 casualties of the 4,000 legionnaires who took part.

In September 1915 another Legion battalion of 1,600 men was sent against Navarin Farm, a German machine-gun post. The sweeping fire laid them dead and wounded in rows, and in an effort to inspire them a legion trumpeter sounded *Boudin*. It produced the old Legion spirit, but bravery was not enough against the German machine-guns, and casualties were more than eight hundred.

By November 1915 Legion casualties had been so heavy, with fewer recruits coming forward, that all the Legion *régiments de marche* in France were fused into one unit, the Régiment de Marche de la Légion, of three battalions; under this title they served for the rest of the war in the Moroccan Division.

Some Legion battles were as fierce and protracted as any of the war. In April 1917, for instance, the Régiment de Marche de la Légion was ordered to take Auberville, part of the German line between Rheims and Soissons. In a hand-to-hand fight, that lasted for six days and nights, the Legion and Germans struggled in the mud and muck and the Legion took 2 kilometres of ground, using fifty thousand grenades in the fight. The battle ended only because both sides were exhausted and had run out of grenades.

Legionnaires had one more hazard than other soldiers because, unintentionally, they shot one another in the dark and were shot by their allies. The trouble was that the legionnaires, being of different nationalities, had no characteristic way of running or walking. Veteran soldiers, who could usually tell the nationality of a shadowy figure, were inclined to shoot when they were uncertain. Some German legionnaires were shot by French troops because they could not help looking like Germans in the dark.

A few Legion *sous-officiers* were deliberately shot. One was Adjudant Pelotti, a Corsican—'a thick-set, coarse little swine with homosexual tendencies'—according to an American legionnaire.[42] Pelotti had been harassing a big, mild legionnaire, Marco; when Marco ignored the sly pats and pinches Pelotti made his life hell. One night as the platoon waited for its relief to arrive Marco, who had a good, trained voice, burst into song. Pelotti rushed forward, and shoved his revolver into Marco's ribs. '*Sacre cabotin de bordel* —singing again! Stop that bloody row or I'll blow your liver through your backbone!'

Marco was silent, but Pelotti continued with his abuse and threats. Somewhere behind Pelotti there were three ominous clicks, the noise of breech bolts being snapped as three cartridges were loaded.

91

Pelotti hurled himself out of danger. It was too easy for somebody to stumble and have a rifle to go off 'by accident' in the dark, muddy trenches. The hint was enough.

Once during rifle inspection a victim of Pelotti's persecutions went *cafard*, and fired at him point-blank but missed the adjutant and killed a corporal standing near by. One night Pelotti took out a reconnaissance patrol. He advanced a certain distance into no man's land and ordered them to proceed while he waited for them. Half an hour later he crawled back, dying, with three French bullets in him. The rest of his patrol had lost their bearings and mistaken him for a German outpost. At least that was their story, and they stuck to it.

One Legion battalion had a series of adventures in the Near East, beginning with the Gallipoli campaign, April–December 1915. By mid June the Turks had so badly mauled them that only a hundred men survived. Partly reinforced, the battalion was sent to Serbia, where it was the prop of the Serbian retreat under Bulgarian pressure. In 1916, when the Serbians advanced, the Legion battalion was the only infantry which could stand the pace, and marched into Monastir with the Serbian *cavalry*. But with so many sick and wounded the battalion was disbanded at the end of 1917.

In April 1917 the Legion 'task force' in France was taken over by Colonel Rollet, a small, fiery and efficient old-type Legion officer with a fan-shaped beard. But at the age of forty-two Rollet, with twenty years' service in the Legion behind him, was anything but old-fashioned. . . . It was a shrewd appointment, for Rollet was loved by these rough men and their morale soon became high—and their prestige higher. Unorthodox, even eccentric, Rollet often puzzled his men. He would help a drunken legionnaire back to barracks and smuggle him past the guard, yet would deal severely with a man brought up on some trivial charge. He would sentence a legionnaire to detention, which meant that the man had no pay, so Rollet would lend him money to send home to his family. Rollet never wore a shirt under his tunic; false cuffs were kept in place with string attached to the armholes of his tunic. When they broke loose at ceremonial moments everybody except Rollet was embarrassed.

Legionnaires affectionately called him 'Captain Espadrilles' because on parade, standing behind a ceremonial table or rail, he wore carpet slippers. Legionnaires liked eccentric officers and Rollet reciprocated by making these men feel like members of the world's most exclusive club. A month after he took command the French Army mutinied. In this crisis Rollet assembled his officers and announced: 'You are all based in and around Mourmelon, where many of the mutineers are heading. The disease should not touch the Legion. Establish look-out posts on all roads leading to Mourmelon and bar the road to any troops not under proper command. If mutinous troops try to force entry into the camp, stop them.'

One officer spoke for all. 'How do you mean, mon colonel, stop them?'

'I mean, just stop them,' Rollet said patiently. 'They are not enemies. They are Frenchmen, misguided, but Frenchmen. And our legionnaires are Frenchmen too, by all the blood they have shed.'

A significant incident came out of this order. Next morning Lieutenant Fernand Maire rode on a tour of his outposts and found two legionnaires leaning against a tree as they faced fifteen French deserters, sitting on the side of the road. The legionnaires smartly presented arms. Maire demanded to know what was going on.

One legionnaire, a Slav, explained through a cascade of obscenities, that he had first shown the deserters his muscles and then he and his comrade had held them at bayonet point. Maire asked the other legionnaire, an American still with the Legion, for his comments. 'Nothing much to say,' he said. 'Just that it's time these goddam Frenchmen know what we mean by the word legionnaire.'

Lieutenant Maire ordered the dangerously sullen men to their feet. 'It is clear that you are not passing here,' he said. 'There are two legionnaires stopping you. You don't mess about with a legionnaire, even less with two. Now get back to your base.'

The impassive legionnaires faced out the deserters, who finally fragmented and shuffled off. It seems hardly necessary to say that no legionnaire took part in the great mutiny.

Under Rollet, the RMLE became more efficient, and in the battle of Cumiers they took more than two miles of territory for 350 casualties—high but acceptable in those bloody days. Rollet led the RMLE detachment which took part in the Bastille Day celebrations in Paris on 14th July 1917. The President pinned the Médaille Militaire to the Legion Colour, thus making it the most decorated one in the French Army; it now had six decorations.

They did not seem too many to compensate for the terrible casualties and tragedies. An officer, the Marquis de Montesquieu, seeing a German white flag, took eight legionnaires to the spot— and all died in a German ambush.

Other legionnaires were luckier. A detachment was sent to the United States on a 'circus tour' to whip up more war fervour. Feted and praised, these tough men were given a reception such as they had never had before. Their journal, *Képi Blanc*, noted that it was the first time legionnaires had come back fatigued from eating too well and being too well received.

Another bloody but important battle flared up in 1918 during the last major German offensive of the war. The Legion was not engaged until 24th April, at Hangard Wood, when it attempted to stop a violent German attack. Casualties in one battalion were so heavy that all the officers were hit. A corporal commanded the remnants of one company and a legionnaire another. When the other two Legion battalions came up in support a five-hour fight ensued, with the Legion trying desperately to prevent the Germans from taking the Amiens road. They did do—at a cost of 850 casualties. The reward —another decoration on the colour.

The Legion's last battle of the war was at Allemany—when companies were down to fifty, some without officers. In this thirteen-day battle to break the Hindenburg Line the RMLE lost 275 killed and 1,500 wounded; about 700 legionnaires stayed on their feet, many of them barely so.

Manuel Moyet of Alabama, one of the last Americans with the Legion, was the hero of one of its last exploits. His citation for the Croix de Guerre was concise. 'Legionnaire Moyet withstood effectively enemy machine-guns with his automatic rifle. . . . Afterwards he individually broke up several counter-attacks.' Badly wounded, Moyet wrote from hospital: 'After the war it is going to be the greatest honour to have served with the Foreign Legion. . . . The spirit of the Legion is wonderful, although many of the most famous legionnaires are dead. Should I live to be a hundred I shall never forget a man of my section who, mortally wounded, lay between the lines shouting, "Vive la France. Vive la Légion!" '[43]

No fewer than 42,883 legionnaires passed through the Legion's ranks in Europe; about 6,250 were French. They lost 115 officers and 5,172 legionnaires killed while nearly 500 officers and 30,000 men were wounded or missing.

In some ways the war went on. Geoffrey Bocca tells the almost bizarre story of a young American legionnaire, one of many who frequented a certain bordello in Paris. This soldier often wrote home to his parents about his 'great friend'—the madame of the bordello —at whose charming house on the Rue de Brey he had met some very nice young ladies. His letters were full of piquant ambiguities which he shared with the madame over wine and laughter. When the legionnaire went to his death in the Champagne fighting, madame and her girls sighed sadly yet again and went on with their war work.

After the war madame received a letter from the dead soldier's parents to say that they were visiting France to see their son's grave and would like to thank the lady who had been so kind to him. The startled madame prepared for them. She sent her girls on holiday, induced the police to let her remove the red light from her door, and stacked all the glittering trappings of the bordello into a couple of rooms and locked them. Then she borrowed a mass of respectable middle-class furniture from her sister in the provinces.

Madame entertained the American parents to tea in her very correct house, then accompanied them on their search of the military cemeteries in Champagne. The three of them wept together over the legionnaire's grave—and the madame's tears were as genuine as those of the parents.[44]

Those legionnaires who survived, and all those who came after them, were given the distinction of wearing a green and gold lanyard, the colours of the ribbon of the Médaille Militaire, France's highest decoration for bravery. Colonel Rollet became the Legion's first Inspector-General, but was more pleased with the title the legionnaires bestowed upon him—'Father of the Legion'. He died at Sidi Bel-Abbes, as he had always wanted, in 1941.

Chapter 12

The 'Golden' Age

To an idealist, the Legion said, in effect, 'But what you are doing *is* worth-
while. War *is* glorious. Courage in the face of overwhelming odds *is* the
greatest virtue a man can possess.' And then ... the Legion added, in
effect, 'Consider our glorious history. As you ponder it, you will find the
pains of the moment charmed away.' Charles Mercer, in *The Foreign
Legion.*

The period between 1919 and 1939 was the golden age of the French
Foreign Legion, if we assume 'golden' to mean adventure and
conquest, widespread fighting and the building of Legion reputation.
These were the decades of the most famous legionnaires, other than
those of Camerone and the few others who had established themselves as public figures among anonymous individuals.

With World War I over, recruits came forward in large numbers,
with Germans predominating. We have the bitter testimony of
Maurice Magnus, a former manager of the great Isadora Duncan,
who had enlisted in the Legion in North Africa in 1914. He had hoped
to get to the European war but was kept in Africa. 'The Legion,'
he wrote, 'is German, German food, German manners, German
discipline, German militarism, German arrogance, German insolence
and German arbitrariness. Every sergeant-major but one is a German. Every sergeant but two is a German. The severity of punishments is German. It is a German regiment of the lowest type
transferred to Africa.' [45] This unequivocal criticism in part reflects
Magnus's unhappy experiences in the Legion—he was a confessed
homosexual—but his generalizations had a lot of truth.

It was understandable that many Germans and their allies would
join the Legion after the war; Germany had too few jobs for them.
In any case some Germans, embittered by defeat, found solace in
fighting the Arabs. Many White Russians, some of whom had held
high rank in the Imperial Russian Army, also found a last refuge in
the Legion.

By 1922 Captain Fernand Marie Maire—the officer who had

96

confronted the deserters in France—had become the beau ideal of the French Foreign Legion in North Africa. He could make his natural swagger look dignified, he was gentle and courteous but as hard as Meknes parade ground. His breast was ablaze with battle awards, which the flowing white Arab cape did not hide. His scarlet kepi gave him a regal look and he went into battle armed only with a cane 'to set an example'. Maire's great trouble at this time was that of many a Legion officer before him—the difficulty of welding into a fighting force a motley collection of men, many of whom had decided they did not want to be in the Legion at all. In Casablanca, Oran and Algiers gangs of deserters had formed into dangerous bands, especially the Russians. Most were looking for ways of getting smuggled out of Africa. The Legion was acquiring a bad reputation and Captain Maire of the 1st Regiment did something about it.

He personally rode out to visit all the friendly local Moroccan chiefs, then invited them to a Legion march-past and a feast. Finally he made a speech, the gist of which was: 'There are many rebellious and violent tribes in Morocco and if the French Army becomes weak we cannot protect you from these dangerous men, who will assuredly despoil your harems. . . . I cannot afford to lose men from the Legion. Should you or your men bring me in a deserter you will receive a reward of twenty francs. But if you bring me in merely the head of a deserter the reward will be one hundred francs.' Every legionnaire in Meknes knew about the offer within minutes.

Maire's offer was low. For most of the Legion's time in Algeria there was a reward of fifty thousand francs for the capture of a legionnaire who had deserted. For an Arab this was a fortune and he would do anything to get the reward—even murder for it. From instinct, as officers and NCOs frequently told recruits, an Arab could smell out a deserting legionnaire at a distance of 2 kilometres.

About this time another flamboyant officer arrived in Meknes to join the 3rd Regiment. The Legion's most regally illustrious member, he was Prince Aage of Denmark, nephew of the King of Denmark and the King of England and of the late Czar of Russia, cousin to almost every prince in Europe and great-grandson of Louis Philippe, founder of the Legion. His mother was Princess Marie of Orleans. Having, in 1914, married a commoner and a Catholic Aage had renounced his claims to the Danish throne and taken his bride to Algiers for their honeymoon. The marriage was not successful, and to complete his personal misfortunes Aage's father had lost nearly all his money in a bank failure. One brother married a Swedish princess, two married American heiresses to millions. Aage had no doubt of *his* course. As a boy at Eton he had read all there was to read about the Legion; now, at thirty-five, tall and still slim, he joined it.

Equally outstanding as Maire and Aage was Major Zinovi Pechkoff, Maxim Gorki's son. The one-armed Pechkoff was a remarkable man by any standards. Refusing any help to mount his horse, he would take the reins in his teeth, put his foot in the stirrup then, gripping the crupper in his right hand—the only one—he pulled himself into the saddle. He was a tough officer and he had his reasons for toughness. 'Even when there was no work to be done, I worked the men furiously,' he said. 'I forced them to do all manner of arduous and even unnecessary labours. As long as they grumbled and cursed me, I knew everything was all right. I was, above all, anxious that they should not become bored or inert, which would make them prey to the *cafard*.'

Ward Price said that in talking with Pechkoff he had come to appreciate the 'almost religious character of this institution, the Legion. And when Major Pechkoff, his eyes shining with faith, speaks of his men with . . . human and direct simplicity his friends think: an Apostle'.[46]

Aage and Pechkoff were great friends, and one night at the Hôtel du Maroc in Fez they dismissed the orchestra and played Arab music together, beautifully, for more than an hour.

Strong again, the French determined on pacification of Morocco. They did not fully realize how difficult a task they had, for nobody had yet assessed the threat posed by the most influential Moroccan leader, Abd El-Krim. Secure in the heart of the Riff Mountains, Krim, helped by a few Europeans and some Legion deserters, trained his men to fight the French with weapons, including captured French and Spanish artillery pieces and machine-guns. Krim even had two aircraft, valuable for reconnaissance in that difficult country.

Leaders and prophets among the tribes south of the Riff Mountains were becoming increasingly hostile, and many 'show the flag' patrols were ordered. A corporal and five men from Captain Maire's company were sent, in 1922, to a restless area to patrol during the day heat while observing tribal activities and to return at nightfall. In an area considered pacified the patrol met three Berber shepherds, who offered hot black coffee. The soldiers piled their rifles, as if in a drill; the Berbers then drew knives and savagely hacked away at the legionnaires. One, wounded in the stomach and twice hit by bullets fired from the legionnaires' captured rifles, reached the company post. Maire sent out a strong detachment. They found the dead legionnaires, all decapitated and with heads transposed. The hands had been cut off at the wrists, shuffled out of order and set in the sand in an attitude of prayer.

Veteran officers and *sous-officiers* warned the legionnaires, new to this kind of war, of the enemy's ruses, but not all listened attentively enough. A party of Berbers would crawl at night to a Legion outpost and one would toss a stone near a sentry. As the legionnaire raised his head a Berber would flick a rope around his neck. Sometimes the Berbers would kill every sentry this way and vanish. The effect on Legion morale was devastating. They seldom took Arab prisoners and never Berbers because they refused to be taken; legionnaires trying to help Berbers screaming with pain from wounds were themselves shot or stabbed.

The normal procedure with prisoners was for a sentry to keep guard by moving freely among them, but on one occasion a different method was adopted. It earned for Gabez the name of 'The Bloody Oasis'.

Some Arab prisoners had been handcuffed when captured. These handcuffs had long chains, so that when a man was tied to a tree he had room to sit down and to walk a few paces. One night seven prisoners were tied to seven trees, watched by seven sentries. In the morning there were no prisoners—their handcuffs hung limp from the trees—and the seven sentries were lying each at the foot of a tree and with their throats cut so that the heads were practically severed: seven men in handcuffs watched by seven men with revolvers in a desert miles from any possible means of assistance. Legionnaire Waterhouse heard his lieutenant say, 'It is a complete mystery and a bad business for the Legion. It is a disgrace for any prisoner to escape us, and doubly so under these circumstances. The sentries are dead —and if they were not, they would have been shot this morning— and yet their death has robbed us of an explanation.'

To Waterhouse the explanation was simple. The sentries fell asleep and a passing tribe slew them as they slept and freed the men. But ever after legionnaires feared a posting to Gabez.[47]

Some disasters of greater magnitude were caused by sheer incompetency of Intelligence or over-confidence by generals. At Skoura in May 1922 a general sent 253 legionnaires, under Captain Maire, to do a job that needed 3,000 soldiers—at a time when 3,000 were immediately available. The force was routed; 17 were killed, 61 were wounded and another 18 captured and burned alive. Maire, losing his scarlet kepi in the *mêleé*, charged unarmed back through the tribesmen to retrieve it—and lived.

Aage was present at another slaughter on 24th June 1923 in a mountain pass near El Mers, and lived to write about as bizarre an incident as anything in war. A Belgian lieutenant, Mollenbeek, fell dead, and at once another Belgian veteran, Legionnaire Vandenbroek, rushed to bring the lieutenant to cover. He was riddled with bullets and fell near the dead officer. The column suffered two hundred casualties before radio messages brought help, then Aage had time to collect the papers of the dead Belgians. In both wallets he found a photograph of the same woman, though that in Mollenbeek's wallet showed her as much older. Aage, with access to people in influential positions, found that Vandenbroek was Mollenbeek's father, though neither knew of the other's existence in the Legion.

About 1898 Vandenbroek, desperately in love, had married Marie Mollenbeek in Brussels, but before long Marie was having affairs with other men, and when Vandenbroek caught her in bed with one of them she laughed at him. His world broken, Vandenbroek found sanctuary in the Legion, where he became known for his never-smiling face, though he was a good soldier. In Brussels Marie, with plenty of lovers, soon forgot about him and adopted her maiden name. Her son became a professional officer, served with the Belgians during World War I and later joined the Legion.[48] In the Legion such a story as the father and son who fell together would not necessarily be unique.

Both Arabs and French went on a more general offensive, and fighting was costly in casualties; three Legion battalion commanders were wounded. Krim's Moslems were savage opponents, and as always the legionnaires dreaded capture, the inevitable torture and a lingering death. Every legionnaire kept a last bullet in his pocket for himself.

At Tichoukt Mountain a Legion detachment, escorting a ration convoy, fought a Camerone-like battle. No survivors this time; the party was wiped out to a man. At Tseghouchen a Legion battalion fought for twelve hours before repelling a force three times its own numbers. Krim's first major offensive, in April 1924, was at first devastatingly successful. He quickly crushed the thin Legion forces and reached the gates of Fez. The French were paying the price for Spanish military inefficiency. The whole Spanish army had collapsed before Krim and he had mountains of weapons and equipment with which to fight the French.

But the Legion officers sensed that he had another more sinister asset, because the Riffians had improved as soldiers; they were better at setting and avoiding ambushes, they had learnt to fire the captured Spanish artillery. Somebody was training them. There were rumours of a mysterious personality, El Hadj Aleman, who left a card inscribed 'El Hadj' pinned to the tunics of dead legionnaires. Unusually such bodies were not mutilated. Dressed as a mounted Legion officer, El Hadj would visit an isolated Legion fort to be at once admitted and entertained by the few officers, always eager to see a new face. The garrison would wake in the morning to find rifles and ammunition—and the visiting officer—missing. But he would leave his card conspicuously displayed.

It took French Intelligence some months to find out that El Hadj was a deserter legionnaire—Otto Klems, a German from Düsseldorf, formerly a professional burglar and footloose adventuer. Reaching Morocco in 1912 he joined the Legion and his strength and intelligence soon made him a *sous-officier*. Despite his wanderings, Klems had remained very much a German and hated the French. When the war broke out in 1914 he had a problem: return to Germany and go to prison for several crimes the police knew about or stay in the Legion. He chose the Legion, which classed him as too untrustworthy to be sent to France, so he spent the war in Morocco. He was a harsh *sous-officier* of the 'Beau Geste' type and he openly cheered news of German victories in Europe.

Still, his allegiance was to the Legion flag and in campaigns against the Berbers and Bedouins he distinguished himself, was several times decorated and towards the end of the war he was commissioned as an artillery lieutenant. Klems was distressed by the German defeat in Europe, but he was in any case bored with the Legion. Complex, ambitious, curious, he thought about defecting to the Berbers, but this was not a light decision. Other men from the French and Spanish Foreign Legions who had gone over lived miserable half-lives.

In Fez one night in 1920, during a Legion officers' dinner at the Hôtel du Maroc, a drunken French captain called Klems a 'Boche'. Klems savagely knocked him down. To strike a superior officer was a heinous Legion crime, so Klems hurried out and rode back to his post where he gathered as many automatic weapons as possible, a peace-offering to the Riffs, and rode for the hills.

It was a hazardous venture. A tribe of wild Berbers found him, tied him up and discussed ways in which they might kill him slowly. Fluent in the Berber tongue, Klems told his captors that the weapons proved he was a friend to the Moslems, that he could show them how to fight the French. The tribal leader offered him life if he adopted the Moslem faith, which meant being circumcised by a filthy Arab knife in the flickering light of tallow strips. Klems went through this ordeal, was added to the tribe's slaves, suffered beatings and humiliations—and waited.

101

While herding sheep one day he saw a captured French officer brought in and watched as the women dug a grave for him. The approaching execution meant nothing to Klems, but then he saw that the 'grave' was a post-hole type and that the women were bringing out pots of honey. Klems knew what this meant. The officer was to be buried up to his neck and his head covered in honey to attract insects and animals. Klems, as Prince Aage was to say later, 'played the game according to the rules'. This preparation for torture sent him berserk; he beat the women away from the Frenchman, but the tribesmen then overpowered him and flogged him into unconsciousness. At least he did not see the French officer die.

Klems's redemption came when he was allowed to marry the chief's daughter, a girl of fifteen; this automatically made him a chief with horses, sheep and servants. By now, in 1923, Abd El-Krim had heard of Klems and he sent for him. Krim was pleased to hear of Klems's skill with guns and maps, and even more of his ability as a photographer. He gave Klems a captured Spanish camera and told him to photograph the Riff war against the French for which he was then preparing. Promoted to Krim's chief-of-staff and personal secretary, Klems drilled whole battalions of Riffs. Wearing an orange turban, and conspicuous by his great black beard and camera, he was given the red-carpet treatment he had always wanted. He took several wives, gave them all children and acquired property.

Doing what he could to make life more bearable for prisoners, he saved several from castration. He rarely refused to meet journalists, and to the American, Vincent Sheean, he expounded his philosophy, 'This is my adopted country and I am happy here. I was a German. Now I am a Riff. As long as the Sultan [Krim] is in power I am a rich man. In fighting, I like to kill people, especially Frenchmen.'[49]

Krim seemed invincible, and the French commander-in-chief, Marshal Lyautey, now seventy-one, leaned more and more heavily on his legionnaires. At every Legion post parades were held to select the fittest men for front-line action, but in May 1925 Krim was still keeping the Legion in retreat. At Astar, in June, the Arabs besieged an important post, and a company led by Pechkoff made a forced march to relieve it. Pechkoff retook the place and found a garrison of three men still able to fight. The sergeant at Astar had been captured; the legionnaires found him tortured to death.

The garrison of Mediouna, running out of food and ammunition, formed up Legion fashion and tried to break through the Riff besiegers. Pechkoff's scouts from their camp at Taounate picked up three survivors. His cavalry patrols observed the fort from a close but safe distance and saw no sign of life. Pechkoff, the much-wounded veteran, wrote later, 'We could not look at each other because we were filled with horror; the horror of losing our youngest and best, some of the most wonderful legionnaires we had. Their presence was still among us. We could see their gay and bright faces! We could hear their laughter and their jokes. . . .'[50] It did not take much imagination to see the legionnaires as they fought to stop themselves being taken alive.

Krim was checked, but he regrouped, brought in more artillery and European advisers and began a second offensive in April 1925. French Intelligence had badly underestimated his strength; he had thirty thousand well-armed soldiers and his objective was elimination of the sixty-six Legion blockhouses of the Taza Corridor. His men crushed nine of them and more than thirty had to be evacuated. The French rushed reinforcements from Algeria, with two Legion battalions as the main striking force, and with outstanding junior leadership and rank and file courage they recaptured many of the blockhouses.

But they had some ghastly failures. Ordered to retake Mediouna Hill, a Legion battalion made a night march with an advance guard of sixty. Bumping into enemy opposition, and assuming it to be an outpost, the advance guard attacked with bayonets and grenades. In fact they had encountered the main enemy position. The battalion halted and waited for information; three survivors brought back the bad news. The battalion at once attacked up the slopes, but the position had been abandoned; all they found were fifty-seven mutilated Legion corpses.

The French and Spanish took too long to join forces and build up strength for a campaign, but when they did the French alone had three hundred thousand men, and Marshal Pétain, the hero of Verdun, had been given command. The Riffs had become over-confident and weakened by their successes; many tribes had gone home to enjoy their booty.

The French-Spanish offensive got going in the spring of 1926, and Krim surrendered his forces on 26th May. The French began a village-by-village, hovel-by-hovel hunt for Klems, said to have been wounded in the fighting. Leaflets and photographs by the thousand were distributed offering a reward for El Hadj Aleman. For six months there was no news, until a woman walked into a Legion company's camp near Messaoud, deep in the Riff Mountains. Refusing to give her name, she said that Hadj was ill and in hiding in a nearby cave; she wanted the reward.

The lieutenant posted his men then, revolver drawn, stood near the cave entrance and shouted to Klems to come out with his hands up. There was no movement until the officer threatened to send his men in shooting. Then out hobbled a filthy, fever-ridden, abscess-covered skeleton, blinking and shaking. 'You fought a good fight and the Legion respects you, Klems,' the lieutenant said. 'Don't be frightened.'

Krim and Klems, the two great Riff figures, had a better end than many people thought they deserved. Krim was exiled to the Indian Ocean island of Réunion with his two favourite wives, some servants and a pension of about £500 a month. In 1947, after twenty-one years on Réunion, the French released him, when he said he wanted to live out his life on the Riviera. He jumped ship at Suez and was a militant Arab hero in Egypt until he died in February 1963, aged sixty-five.

Klems was tried by a French Army war council in February 1927 and, still unwell, was carried into court on a stretcher. His defence was that he had joined the Riffs while they were fighting only the Spaniards, and that by the time the French entered the war he was a Moslem; he could not, therefore, be a traitor since as a naturalized Arab he was simply fighting for the freedom of his country.

Predictably the French sentenced him to death, but American public opinion was in his favour through the press reports of Vincent Sheean and others. The German Foreign Office appealed on his behalf and in Paris the French Communists demonstrated for him. His sentence was commuted to seven years on Devil's Island, but this too was a face-saving device. The French quietly released him and told him to get out of North Africa and stay out. By now he was such a colourful figure that Sigmund Romberg put his adventures to music in *The Desert Song*; the hero, the Red Shadow, is based on Klems.

Back in Germany Klems could find no way of earning a living except by housebreaking. In August 1929 in Berlin he was held on suspicion and locked up for the night while inquiries were made. Klems, the great Riff chieftain, now a social outcast, could face no more ignominy; he cut his wrists with a penknife and the blood he had not already shed for the Legion or for the Riffs poured onto the German floor.

While Klems was coming to the end of his hectic life the Legion was settling down to its traditional dual role—building roads and blockhouses and fighting off raiding bands of Arabs. There was no mistaking the Legion forts scattered throughout Algeria, Morocco and Tunisia—small and square-shaped with squat towers at each corner and parapeted walls. Most were built on hilltops and therefore had a water supply problem. In some ways the period from about 1928 to 1932 was a low point in Legion history, for legionnaires found themselves lent or hired out to local authorities as labourers to work on farms and various projects. This degeneration into a labour corps damaged morale, but some groups of legionnaires accomplished tremendous feats.

Probably the most remarkable was the mile-long 'Tunnel des Legionnaires', cut through solid rock between Midelt and Erfoud in the Atlas Mountains in 1928. At the entrance the Pioneer and Sapper Company of the 3rd Regiment carved their seven-flamed grenade and an inscription—'The mountain barred the road to us. The order was given to pass nonetheless. The Legion executed it. November 27–May 1928.' Appended were the names of the legionnaires who had done the job. They are significant in their origin: Michez, Wagner, Dippulter, Strohschein, Ferraza, Kupras, Lopez, Schubert, Schneider, Picknick, Grunewald, Lusiardi, Golasowski, Laloy, Iarasko, Schubert, Rotenburg, Smirny, Brietenberger, Beucher, Schelzer, Zasada, Bucher, Daniel, Iedlicka, Becker, Ascaso, Rhonisch, Bejer, Pollak, Borges, Wagner, Picoueur, Charliur, Klein, Weimann.

After independence in 1962 the Moroccans defaced the badge, removed the names and gave the tunnel an Arabic name; it was a shabby way to treat the work of those legionnaires.

In retrospect it is easy to see that legionnaires of all ranks were acquiring a maturity of pride, largely the work of General Rollet who strove to keep *esprit de corps* high even when Army HQ was regarding the Legion as basically a pick-and-shovel brigade. Officers took their cue from Rollet and Maire, Pechkoff and Aage and considered themselves above any law but Legion law. Captain Jansen, on a motoring holiday in France in 1928, knocked down and killed a pedestrian. At the police station the police asked for his fingerprints. 'No Legion officer need ever be printed!' Jansen said.

The inspector of police said, 'I am sorry, Captain, but in a case like this fingerprinting is compulsory.'

'We can find a way around that,' Jansen said calmly, and pressed all ten finger-ends on the police station stove, obliterating the whorls.

During the almost ceaseless activity in North Africa there had been a bloody Legion sideshow in Syria, which then included what is now the Lebanon. After World War I the whole area had become a French mandate and the French hoped that they would be welcomed after the long, oppressive Turkish occupation of the area. They were startled when the Druse tribes rebelled. Mountain people, brave and warlike, the Druse were fanatical Mohammedans, and all their enemies had found them difficult to handle. French tactics were to confine the Druse to the hills, so a Legion battalion was sent to block the major route out. The policy worked for a time, but on 16th September 1922 three thousand Druse assembled for a three-pronged attack on the Legion position. Despite the arrival of reinforcements and, next morning, machine-gunning from the air, the Druse fought relentlessly. They faded away on the night of the 17th, leaving 500 of their men dead and another 500 too badly wounded to escape. The Legion lost 47 killed and 83 wounded.

An epic of the Syrian campaign was the battle at Rachaya fort, where a Legion cavalry squadron fought a four-day action—an astonishing display of resistance which deserves to be better known. On the evening of 20th November 1925, three thousand Druse attacked as the legionnaires were watering their horses. The attack was unexpected, but the men manned the walls and held off the main assault made as dusk fell. That night the Druse broke into the fort and after desperate fighting the legionnaires abandoned part of the defences. At dawn they bayonet-charged the Druse and re-captured some of the lost parts of the fort. Fighting was incessant for three days and one Druse assault after another was checked. The officer commanding sent off carrier pigeons with messages asking for help. Help was certainly needed, though on the third day the legionnaires, with bomb and bayonet, cleared the Druse survivors from the fort. But now the legionnaires had little energy and the fort was littered with dead and dying. No grenades remained and ammunition was down to fifteen rounds a man on the fourth day. As in North Africa, each legionnaire kept a last round for himself; the Druse women were as cruel in their tortures as the Tuareg and Riffs.

The Legion commander, assessing the situation as a Camerone crisis, made arrangements for a final charge into the mass of Druse if no relief force arrived as night fell. Late that afternoon a relief column forced its way through and found half the squadron dead and many others wounded. After many a patrol action of the type the Legion knew so well in North Africa, Syria was peaceful enough by 1927. The Legion, of course, turned to building roads and bridges.

The Legion was even less popular in Syria than anywhere else it had fought, mostly because of the *démerdez-vous* policy. For instance, firewood was supposed to come in by railroad, but it never did arrive, so the legionnaires foraged for it and the villages suffered. The men would 'borrow' or take away with promises to bring the equivalent back, which they neither would nor could do. Legionnaire Doty (known as Gilbert Clare) stole a gate from a main street in broad daylight. 'We dug up fence posts in the darkness without asking permission. One of our men came in one night with an entire door, which he had unhinged without the owner's knowledge. They were sleeping at the very moment innocently in a house without a door. . . .

'There never existed anywhere any body of men more efficient for the work there was to do. . . . The tradition is that in such a foray, all that is food goes to everyone and is shared among the kitchens of the different outfits. But if anything else is found, that is the finder's business: he keeps it. Squads of men went about beating down doors with the butts of their rifles, flowing into the houses. You can tell of their progress through the house by the crash of glass and crockery, and the crash of furniture being destroyed.

'It was a wealthy village; there seemed to be many plate-glass mirrors; the Legionnaires would attack them with the same joy one sometimes sees in firemen under similar circumstances. Then with everything reduced to kindling inside, they'd pour out, laden with linens and sometimes silks, with bracelets and spangles and knick-knacks, with great jars of honey and blocks of dried raisins, with watches and with clocks, with God knows what. Outside, the streets ran with herded sheep and goats, with donkeys and mules and bullocks. One man had found a blooded mare, another a fine stallion. Together with the *adjudant-chef* of the company, I was after chicken, ducks and geese. I had finally twenty-nine chickens and one goose all in one huge chaplet, and a donkey to carry them.

'Meanwhile Budney [a comrade] taken along by the *adjudant-chef* of the battalion, was busy at another matter. The two men, going into each house successively after the looters were through, were pouring kerosene over the floors and the walls and touching a match to it. Then, looking like some migrating pastoral people of bygone days on the move, we marched off carrying with us our loot, driving before us our cattle, behind us the village was starting to burn fiercely under great clouds of smoke.'[51]

Doty, with an English legionnaire, Harvey, and two Germans, Weisser and Lass, deserted after Doty had been in the Legion less than a year. Doty's lame excuse was that he had *cafard*. Completely without resourcefulness, the group botched the job and were caught. Doty was at first sentenced to be shot—he had, after all, deserted while his unit was in action—but was reprieved after official American agitation and repeated appeals to the French Minister of War. He spent what he considered 'eight long, weary terrible months in five

107

French prisons'. Colonel Rollet, who interviewed Doty on his release, said, 'Gilbert Clare, vouz avez de la chance.'

What Rollet said in private was more pungent; he had no time for deserters. He subscribed to the old belief that no legionnaire ever let another legionnaire down.

Chapter 13

The Pride and the Passion

'The truth about the Legion is perhaps too simple for the cinema.' General Rollet, Inspector General of the Legion, discussing *Morocco*, the Marlene Dietrich film about the Legion.

By the 1930s Prince Aage, commander of the 1st Battalion, had more public limelight than any other Legion officer. It was hardly enviable in all its facets; he could drink any of his legionnaires under the table but would be on parade next morning spruce and alert. Socialites, film stars and sensation-seekers travelled to Algeria especially to meet the fabulously romantic and handsome legionnaire prince, and many a maiden found her name coupled with his in the gossip columns. Women found him irresistible.

Aage once commanded a remote fort in Morocco to which HQ sent a cageful of homing pigeons for sending messages. Aage presented them to the chef and every man that night had a portion of pigeon-pie. HQ sent an urgent message: Why were none of the pigeons coming back? 'Birds of prey are getting them,' Aage replied. 'Please send shot-guns and we will kill them.' When the shot-guns arrived Aage, his officers and *sous-officiers* hunted table-birds. Aage was a disciplinarian but a good officer to serve under, his men said.

Legion pride showed itself again in 1931 when the corps' great statue to its dead was unveiled in Sidi Bel-Abbes. More than two thousand veteran ex-legionnaires from twenty-seven countries turned up for the unveiling—a superb tribute to the Legion and an implicit rebuke to its denigrators. But not all deaths occurred in battles. On 14th September 1932 a troop-train carrying 500 reinforcements from Sidi Bel-Abbes to Morocco ran off the track at Turenne, killing 56 legionnaires and injuring 217. The Legion built a monument, but Algerian rebels blew it up a generation later.

There was never peace in Morocco, and the Legion learned to live with the fact. Some revolts were serious, as in 1933 when massive tribal uprisings were quelled only after heavy fighting. By 1934 the

French occupied the whole of Morocco, but no legionnaire moved far without his weapons. If a Legion halt was not merely a night bivouac a nomad town would spring up, while the masons and miners built a fort. Greek sutlers, who always knew the Legion's movements, would appear with wine and cigarettes; native pedlars with chickens and eggs; beggars, spies, thieves, native prostitutes. At night many of these people moved back into the hills for the usual nocturnal sniping.

The garrison of one small fort was only twenty men, and it was in such close contact with the Berbers that, although there was a spring less than a mile in front of it, drinking water for the troops was kept in cisterns which could only be replenished by barrels brought on mule-back from a point ten miles in the rear.

An insubordinate German legionnaire in the company was under sentence of transfer to the disciplinary detachment of the Legion at Colomb Béchar. This man, posted one night as sentry on the parapet, deserted to the Berbers. He knew their fierce ways, but had heard that they would spare the life of a deserter who could ransom himself by bringing with him his rifle and a good supply of cartridges. The relief sentry found the post abandoned, and for a month the man was carried on the company roll as 'missing'.

Then one dark night another German sentry on the parapet heard a stealthy, whispered hail from beyond the wire. 'Wer ist's?' asked the startled legionnaire.

'Fritz,' came the reply. 'Don't make any noise. Let me in quietly. I must see the lieutenant.'

The sergeant of the guard cautiously let the man in and took him to the lieutenant in command. In the light of his torch the figure dressed in ragged Berber robes, haggard, half-starved, dirty and unshaven was unmistakably the deserter of a month before. 'Mon lieutenant, there is not a minute to lose!' the man said. 'I have been with the Berbers ever since I deserted. They spared my life because they believed I would tell them the best time and place to attack the post. A hundred of them are lying among the rocks at the foot of the hill. I came on, as they think, to reconnoitre, so that I might warn you. They will rush the fort any moment.'

The garrison, sleeping with their rifles by their side, were called to arms. From the parapet flares went up and, crawling from rock to rock up the slope towards the camp, the grey forms of the Berbers could be seen. Rifle-grenades and machine-guns on the flanking towers of the little post opened up, and after a few moments the only Berbers within sight were dead ones.

The deserter had risked his life several times over to warn his comrades—at the hands of his Berber associates, from the sentries of the fort, who would have been justified in opening fire at the first sound of his furtive hail from the farther side of the entanglement, and again as the established penalty of his crime of desertion in the face of the enemy. He was not charged with desertion, but the original sentence to the disciplinary company still stood.

A convoy stopping at a Legion outpost was a great opportunity for the Legion. While the legionnaire did not usually steal for himself, and never stole from his officers, he took pride in stealing something useful for his unit. A large patrol of mounted Senegalese stayed one night at a fort commanded by Pechkoff.

In the morning as the Senegalese were about to leave they were astonished to see that the harness and the pack-saddles did not fit their animals. Also most of the harness and saddles was old; when they arrived the day before they were all brand new. The mules were the same in number, but some of them had become smaller and weaker during the night. A complete transformation had taken place. Pechkoff might not have known what had happened if the sergeant in charge of the Legion's mules had not mentioned it in his daily report. 'I reported to you a few weeks ago,' he said, 'about the bad condition of our pack equipment. Now I can report to you that nothing is missing and everything is new.'

'What do you mean?' Pechkoff asked. 'We have not received any.'

'No, we have not received any, but we have got it. We had to get it. We asked the commissariat several times to replace our equipment. There was never any answer. Now we have replaced everything. The Senegalese have the old. We have the new.'

Pechkoff reprimanded him, but the sergeant said, 'I did not order it done. The legionnaires did it themselves—each one for his mule. They have been waiting for this chance for a long time. And, after all, it is not for ourselves, it is for the good of the service.'

Pechkoff let it go at that. *Démerdez-vous.* Soldiers of all armies become scroungers, but the Legion would probably win any competition. Nothing was safe when a Legion column passed. It was said that an expert could paint a grey donkey brown in two minutes.

On campaign considerable licence was allowed about kit. Scrupulous though the standard of smartness was on garrison duty, a legionnaire was not worried by kit inspections on active service. He was issued with the correct clothing, but if he lost or otherwise disposed of it no questions were asked. To lighten his pack a man would often sell or throw away his spare pair of boots. When his other pair were out he bought or 'acquired' a pair of native leather sandals, but his unmilitary appearance drew no wrath from officer or sergeant. Ward Price saw one legionnaire on Mount Hamdoun who had even lost his trousers, and was campaigning in his underpants. Provided a man remained fit for military duty his external appearance was of secondary importance.

At this time legionnaires whose behaviour was good enough to escape punishment were entitled to three weeks' annual leave. It had to be spent in Morocco, and since the average legionnaire had no friends, and certainly no money to spend on hotels, Marshal Lyautey, as Resident-General and Commander-in-Chief, had established two rest-houses, at Rabat and at Mogador, where legionnaires could take this 'local leave'. They were wooden bungalows, plainly furnished, but each had a library, and the average soldier was glad enough to spend three quiet weeks as a change from his regular routine of fatigues and drill.[52]

But, as always, on pay days—the 1st and 15th of the month—the garrison cities became Legion property, and wise people kept off the streets, though most of the trouble occurred when legionnaires were in fights with the military police, with Ghoums and Senegalese and other French troops.

Pechkoff found that Germans made the best corporals in the Legion. Russians did not make good corporals because the Russian was always hesitating, and he did not have authority over the men with whom he was living and sharing the same room or tent. He was not firm, Pechkoff said: he was lenient and unsure of his authority. The tone of his voice was not convincing, and even while ordering the men to do something he seemed to doubt as to whether they really must do it. 'But the German, immediately after he is invested with the rank of corporal and the two green stripes are sewn on his sleeve, feels himself a chief and a commander. And he commands his men. He has charge of eight, twelve or sixteen, or whatever number are placed under his immediate command. He will make them obey his orders and, although eating with them from the same plate and sleeping beside them, he will always make them feel that he is their chief. Although these German corporals get just as drunk as their men, a German corporal never drinks with the men of his squad or of his group.'[53]

Pechkoff loved the Legion as another man might love a woman or a monk love Christ. His writing is full of adulation. 'Life with the legionnaires is intense. Weak men perish as a fruit blossom touched by the frost. When one sees the fortified camps, the roads, the bridges that span deep gorges—all constructed by these men during the operations—one has the greatest admiration for their magni-

ficent endurance. Here man feels himself inspired. He goes beyond
himself. His strength is tested every hour, and the harder he works
the more he has courage to continue, and the more confidence he
has in himself.'

His young officers were deeply influenced by Pechkoff's attitudes,
as we see from the brief address made by a lieutenant when his
section buried Legionnaire Velich, their Serbian machine-gunner.
'In the name of the company I salute most humbly and respectfully
the mortal remains of our dear comrade in battle, Velich. He has
been taken away from us in his fourth year of service in Morocco.
He was killed by brigands while doing his duty. Velich died on the
field of honour. In the new life that he is entering, in the Great
Eternity, Velich will be just as great as he was here on earth, where
he kept his word as a legionnaire and died under the flag of the
Legion which bears these words, "Valour and Discipline", "Honour
and Fidelity". Adieu, Velich, rest in peace. The company promises
that it will never forget you.'[54]

Legionnaires were never sentimental about the men they killed,
but many of them were sentimental in other ways. In the early 1930s
one man's enlistment of five years was just about over and he was
anxious to go home. But then his brother died in Sidi Bel-Abbes.
The Legion would have buried him, of course, but the man wanted a
private grave. He had no money, but the bonus paid for a five-year
re-enlistment was equal to the fee. The legionnaire re-enlisted, paid
for the grave and soldiered on. The inscription he had chiselled on
the marble headstone read: 'Erected by one of his 10,000 brothers'.

Time-expired legionnaires about to be discharged developed
strange ambitions. One legionnaire, formerly a captain in an *élite*
Austrian regiment during World War I and later a member of the
General Staff, joined the Legion and became the regimental sergeant-
major of the Legion Cavalry Regiment. A fine soldier, he lived
simply, and in ten years had saved 10,000 francs and applied for his
discharge.

'We shall be sorry to lose you,' said his CO. 'What are you going
to do?'

'Well, sir, I have spent all my spare time studying roulette systems,'
said the *sous-officier*. 'I have discovered an infallible one—not for
breaking the bank; I am not so ambitious—but for winning a steady
profit of 30,000 francs a year. That will be enough for me to live on.'

He was farewelled and went to Monte Carlo. Two months later a
letter from him arrived at regimental headquarters for the commanding officer. 'The system failed,' it said briefly. 'Will you take me
back, even as a trooper?'

113

Relations between officers and men in a corps like the Legion are often very different from those in other armies. There is the documented case, in a garrison town of Morocco, where it was reported to a captain that one of his men, who had a grievance, was boasting in the local bars and cabarets that he would kill him. That night the captain made a round of these places until he located his threatening subordinate, and sat at his table. The other legionnaires present saluted him by rising, the rebellious one pretended not to see him. As the hour of roll-call at the barracks drew near the group prepared to leave. The captain called to his man, 'Wait for me, I need you.'

Some time after the rest had gone the captain led the legionnaire outside and handed over his revolver. 'I want you to escort me back to barracks,' he said. 'People are sometimes attacked by night on those lonely roads outside the town. You are to walk behind me with this pistol and keep a good look out.'

In silence and without incident the two men reached the barracks. The captain took back his revolver. 'You will have eight days' cells for boasting that you would kill your captain,' he said, 'and eight days more for not doing it when you had the chance. A legionnaire should always keep his word. Go and report yourself to the sergeant of the guard.'[55]

Legion discipline, as in this case, could be individualistic and flexible. It could also be almost indulgent. A big Russian legionnaire had been on sentry duty outside the tent of the major commanding a battalion in Meknes and had stolen some of the tent cord for purposes of his own.

Next day, while this man was working at road-building, a sergeant and two men with fixed bayonets took him into custody. He was marched to the major, who accused him of stealing the cord. The Russian admitted it and the major boxed his ears twice. The Russian remained standing to attention. 'As you are my battalion commander I will not defend myself,' he said. The orderly captain, who was present at this interview, then struck him and the Russian knocked the captain down. Normally the punishment for such an offence would be drastic, but the Russian was given only eight days' cells, on the ground that he had acted under extreme provocation.[56]

Another prince had joined the Legion—Dmitri of Georgia—in 1936 the youngest captain in the Legion. Prince Dmitri—and Aage who was weathering faster than he knew—saw another change in the Legion, for as the Spanish Civil War ran its ruinous course the Legion had a great influx of Republican Spaniards, bitter, vengeful and psychologically maladjusted men. Even the *sous-officiers* had difficulty in controlling *these* men; they would gang up and beat an NCO they disliked. They had a taste for sex that disturbed even the most lustful Germans, Belgians and Czechs. The Russian legionnaires, who went about their whoring with a kind of mystical ardour, were appalled at the coarseness of the Spaniards, who practically monopolized the BMCs. While the Germans spent most of their money on drink the Spaniards used almost every cent on girls. They had come from Spain with venereal disease and they infected many girls. Most nights groups of them indulged in compulsive mass masturbation—a rare aberration among most of the central Europeans, who began to detest the Spaniards. In any case, these Spaniards were political animals and the old-time legionnaires cared nothing for politics.

To the Spaniards the oath they took to serve the Legion's flag meant nothing. Nor, apparently, did personal cleanliness, but recollections and reports about cleanliness in the Legion are so conflicting that one must assume that it varied from depot to depot, section to section, man to man. Legionnaire Brian Stuart, who served in the Legion in the late 1930s, did not know of a barracks in Algeria or Morocco, other than the principal depot at Sidi Bel-Abbes, that had a bath. At Ain Sefra Stuart crept downstairs during the night, slipped past the sentries and bathed in the trough used for watering the mules and washing clothes. He never encountered a foot inspection—a frequent event in most armies—and met men who had not washed their feet for years. A sergeant of the 7th Company reprimanded Stuart for washing his feet daily, pointing out that such stupidity would make the feet soft and unfit for marching. Stuart claimed to know of men who had not had a bath in fifteen years. One veteran at Ain Sefra, with thirty years' service and twenty medals, had never had a bath. Stuart found this dirtiness incredible in the face of the Legion's insistence that the linings of sleeves, and pockets of tunics and greatcoats must be scrubbed, yet underclothing could be horribly soiled.[57]

Waterhouse alleged that the barrack walls and beds were crawling with bugs, though Legionnaire McLean, enlisting at the same time, found the barracks, 'well appointed and spotlessly clean'.[58]

Despite the good showing of American legionnaires—the idealists —during World War I the Legion hierarchy considered that Americans made poor Legion material. As with everything else in the Legion, there were exceptions. One young American who did make good in the Legion was Peter Ortiz, born in Paris. His father, Philippe Ortiz, well known in the French art world, was wealthy and had high social standing. The boy, his only son, had been educated in France at a provincial *lycée* and would normally have

115

gone on to a university in that country or the United States. Family affairs in January 1932 took Philippe Ortiz to America. While he was away a letter reached him from his seventeen-year-old son: 'When you get this I shall be on my way to Sidi Bel-Abbes to join the 1st Regiment of the Foreign Legion. I have enlisted for five years in the Legion, and am starting tonight for Marseilles to embark for Algeria. Don't think this is a freak on my part. I have made inquiries about the Legion. I know what I am doing and what I have to expect, and I am not afraid.'

M. Ortiz returned hurriedly to Paris. His conception of the Foreign Legion, like that of most people at the time, was based on the tales of brutality and vice which American hack writers were producing in quantity. M. Ortiz obtained an interview with Marshal Franchet d'Esperey, despairingly told the Marshal of the 'mad' step his son had taken and begged to have him released on the grounds of his age.

'As he is under eighteen, the enlistment was irregular,' the Marshal said, 'and it would be possible to get it annulled, but before you take that step why not travel to Sidi Bel-Abbes where your son will still be under training, to see for yourself whether he is as badly off as you believe.'

M. Ortiz found his son liking the life of the Legion and already proud of its traditions. The father, also a tall, virile man, was infected by the boy's enthusiasm as he visited the Legion museum at Bel-Abbes and when he talked with his son's companions. For the most part, he said later, they were men of courage and character who preferred a hard and even dangerous life with independence to the tedium and steady increase of unemployment in their native lands. Back in Paris, M. Ortiz secured authority to tour all the Legion's garrison towns, camps and even outposts, and for eight months travelled Algeria and Morocco, investigating the life of the corps. He then formed an association called *Les Amis de la Légion Étrangère* ('Friends of the Foreign Legion') at 18 Rue Louis-le-grand, Paris. It had the three Marshals of France as its patrons and a distinguished list of committee members. Its object was to combat slanderous attacks on the Legion and to co-operate with other societies to help the legionnaire, at the end of his service, to start afresh on a civilian career.

The association largely helped to counter the German anti-Legion propaganda which was virulent and persistent at this time. One German pamphlet of 1933 said that 35,000 Germans were serving in the Legion; at that time, the total strength of the Legion was only 10,000. Another pamphlet claimed, 'Out of 35,000 young

Germans at home only 175 die each year, while among the 35,000 in the Foreign Legion the annual mortality is 7,000.'

Another document put the number of German legionnaires at 40,000, and alleged that since 1831, 320,000 Germans had 'sacrificed their lives to the foreign Legion Moloch'. German fugitives from the Legion were constantly to be found, broken in health and poverty-stricken, in the streets of Germany. This was a gross exaggeration, as was the claim of a writer of 1936 that only five out of every hundred legionnaires came out of it alive after the expiration of their contracts.[59]

This was the time when journalists with more imagination than integrity were writing articles about many legionnaires being brazen impostors. It was easy, they said, for a man to enlist in the Legion and claim to have been a general or a minister of state or a prince, because he hid behind a false name. The fact was that since the vast majority of legionnaires wanted anonymity they made no claims of any kind. Prince Aage, Zinovi Pechkoff and Prince Dmitri, the genuine celebrities, could not have hidden their identities. Impostors existed, of course, but they were intra-Legion frauds. And very few could hope to escape exposure for long. One man in Morocco insisted on keeping a clerical tonsure as he was ordained in holy orders. The CO, a pious man, excused the man from all ordinary regimental duties, employed him to teach Latin to his young son and allowed him to hear his wife's confessions when the regular chaplain was absent. The chaplain himself was suspicious, made inquiries and discovered that the legionnaire had never been ordained but had worked as secretary in a seminary, from which he had been dismissed for dishonesty.

Chapter 14

Divided Loyalties of World War II

'Perhaps there is *un vertige collectif d'énergie et d'abnégation* [a collective vertigo of energy and self-denial] which at certain times seizes the Legion and which is incomprehensible to reasonable minds.' Lieutenant Jacques Weygand, in *Legionnaire*.

The 1930s were dying. General Rollet, the one man who could have handled the crisis caused by the influx of Spaniards, had retired in 1935. Fernand Maire, illustrious and legendary as a colonel, left in 1938, the year in which the Legion built something more practical than a memorial. The soldiers dug and concreted and landscaped and built—and produced the finest swimming-pool in North Africa. Even the great British clubs of Cairo could not match it.

The Legion was more than ever conscious of the legionnaire's welfare if only for the pragmatic reason that they wanted him to stay on. Towards the end of his service the legionnaire was encouraged to 'rectify' himself—to declare his true name and nationality and to allow the Legion to check his background. Such rectification carried privileges; the legionnaire could go on leave to his home country. This was a shrewd recruiting device because the legionnaire almost certainly brought back three or four friends as recruits. The enlistment bonus was now 2,000 francs. *Sous-officiers* were permitted to marry 'on the strength' once they had rectified, and could wear civilian clothes in certain circumstances. But since, in 1939, 80 per cent of the Legion's *sous-officiers* were German who liked wearing uniform few availed themselves of this privilege. In that year too 50 per cent of the legionnaires were Spanish, while 25 per cent of the officers were non-French.

The Legion hierarchy became aware, as the tensions of 1939 increased, that a remarkable number of Germans was turning up for recruitment. They were accepted on the usual basis but were watched, as were all key *sous-officiers*. When war broke out several hundred

German legionnaires were at once interned, including all the especially planted agents who were to take control of the Legion by force. To water down the remaining Germans there were soon batches of other foreigners, joining for the same idealistic reasons that had drawn their counterparts of 1914. About six thousand such men, of scores of nationalities, were quickly absorbed into the Legion in Africa and Syria. At the same time foreigners living in France were also recruited, after careful screening, though many of these men did not see service in Africa.

The war brought into the Legion's ranks no less a personality than the Count of Paris, son of the Pretender to the throne of France and Aage's nephew. By French law neither he nor his father was permitted on French soil, but in this emergency he got into the country and interviewed the Prime Minister, Reynaud, who gave his permission for the count to enlist in the Legion under the name of Henry Orliac, a Swiss citizen of Geneva. His identity was supposed to be top secret, but everybody recognized him, and some officers simply did not know how to treat this legionnaire who was a 'crown prince'. Then his father, the Duc de Guise, died at his home in Morocco, so the count was now the Pretender. The Army thought it better if he and the Legion parted. Prince Napoleon, who had also enlisted as an ordinary legionnaire, was also discharged.

Of all the Legion units formed during World War II the most famous was the 13th Demi-Brigade (two instead of three battalions), one of the best-known units in the Allied armies. Aage expected command of the Demi-Brigade and he seemed the perfect choice. He was a Scandinavian and his country had been overrun; he was fifty-three, a good age for a regimental commander, and he was profoundly experienced. But the command went to Colonel Magrin-Vernerey, senior to Aage in age, service and combat experience. More than that he had been wounded seventeen times, and Gallic judgment is influenced by such things.

Aage was disappointed and bitter. Many of his men of the 3rd Battalion at Taza had been posted to the new formation, and at their last march past, after he had saluted the flag, he dismounted and shook the hand of every man in turn. A few weeks later he died. The Legion doctors could not find the reason, but the old legionnaires knew; a simple matter of a broken heart. He was buried at Sidi Bel-Abbes as he had requested.

Formed from volunteers from many Legion units, the 13th was hurriedly assembled for the trip to France where, originally, it was trained for service in Finland, but the destination was changed to Norway. Girls from the BMC assigned to the 13th volunteered to

119

accompany the legionnaires no matter where in Scandinavia they were sent, and were distressed and angry when the offer was declined. Officers explained that the Norwegians would resent their presence, a point the enthusiastic whores could not comprehend, and told them that the legionnaires would have to make the best of whatever was available in Norway, a point they did comprehend and which angered them even more.

Arriving in Norway a month after the German invasion the legionnaires were hurried to Narvik, north of the Arctic Circle. The Legion was not popular in Norway, mainly because of Nazi propaganda; former German legionnaires were induced to broadcast calumny against the newly arrived formation. Even the presence of Norwegians in the Legion's ranks, convenient translators for the Legion, did not make the unit any the more acceptable. Many legionnaires were killed in action on the edge of Narvik and some, their lives spent in heat, froze to death at their posts. Colonel Magrin, knowing that his men needed action, took his two battalions of legionnaires and a Norwegian battalion across Rombas Fiord and in a sharp offensive captured Narvik on 28th May. Because of the strategical demands for troops elsewhere Magrin's men (and the British) did not hold Narvik for long, but the taking of Narvik was the first Allied land victory of the war.

Shipped to France, the Legion had some sound training during the 'phoney war' of the winter of 1939–40, but the German offensive of May 1940 caught them as it caught all the Allied armies. The Legion was thrown into the battle for the Low Countries, and many died there in the midst of acts of bravery which should have won them decorations. One battalion, the 12th, lost two-thirds of its strength when surrounded and then pounded by enemy artillery.

As always, conflict brought out the 'characters', the individualists. One of the most outstanding was Karel Hora, son of a Czech father and Japanese mother. Showing great bravery in an action at Saint-Germain-sur-Meuse, Legionnaire Hora was three times wounded, and because of the onrushing Germans had to be abandoned with other wounded men. Hora knew that as a Czech the Nazis would consider him a traitor and would probably shoot his family in Prague, so he pleaded with a nurse to exchange his identity tag with that of any dead legionnaire. He became Carlos Fernandez of Madrid, serving in the 11th Regiment commanded, as it happened, by Fernand Maire, brought back to the Legion by the war.

When he was fit Hora escaped, and in December 1940 arrived under his own steam at Sidi Bel-Abbes. He was minus two fingers and he had a limp, but he was ready to fight. And he did. He was back in France, at Lyons, when the German Army marched on 11th November 1942 to occupy Vichy France. He escaped across the Pyrenees, was arrested by the Spanish Guardia Civil, jumped from a moving train, was picked up again at Burgos, escaped again, reached Portugal and finally England. Here he was commissioned as a paratroop officer in the Free French Army and parachuted into France to organize the Maquis. He led a contingent of Maquisards and of the Garde Républicaine into action against Germans at Saint Pourcaine, and in the end had eighteen thousand prisoners. Hora was one of the first French soldiers into Paris.

When Captain Hora left the Army and returned to Prague he was an Officer of the Legion of Honour; he held the Croix de Guerre with seven bars, the Croix de Valeur with two bars, the British Military Cross and the American Silver Star. A once-humble *bleu*, he was thirty-eight years old and had become a captain, though at times he exercised a colonel's authority, usually unofficially. We will meet him again.

The cease-fire between the French and German Armies came into effect before the 13th Demi-Brigade could find the success its men clearly sought. It was then near the Channel ports, and Colonel Magrin-Vernerey decided to go to England and continue the fight; about half his men followed. In England he called his formation the 14th Demi-Brigade, but reverted to the original title to defy the Vichy (pro-German) Government's announcement that it had abolished the 13th Demi-Brigade.

The Legion was not given motor vehicles on any scale until World War II. In 1940 they enabled the Legion to form its first mechanized patrol company to police the vast areas of the Sahara. Operating throughout World War II, without ever becoming involved in the war itself, this unit became le Compagnie Saharienne Port de la Légion. Colourfully uniformed and efficient, these legionnaires so impressed Authority that after the war similar units were formed.

The Legion as a body had now to live up to its old policy of 'System-D'—*démerdez-vous*. The Germans wanted the Foreign Legion in Africa disbanded. When this was resisted they insisted on periodic inspections by a German Commission and to the release of certain Germans from it. The Legion officers were too shrewd for the Germans. 'Wanted' legionnaires were quickly sent off to remote posts; when a German inspection was due the German legionnaires were 'unfortunately' on long training exercises—until the Commission had gone. Nevertheless about one thousand Germans were released from the Legion at their own request and were formed into

121

a special battalion by the Germans; they were not allowed to go home to Germany.

After the fall of France the Legion units in France assumed themselves to be still on active service, though this was little more than garrison duty in Algeria and Morocco. But another embarrassing problem arose. About six thousand men had joined for the duration of the war, and when France was defeated they said their war was over and how about their discharge? The Vichy Government refused to release them for the valid reason that most had nowhere to go and, in North Africa, they would be on the loose and a dangerous liability. When the men rejected invitations to accept a standard Legion commitment they were put to work on building the French railway south to Colomb Béchar. They were harshly treated and many died in labour camps which had no connection with the Legion itself.

The two battalions of the 13th Demi-Brigade went first of all, in December 1940, to the French Cameroons, where their presence ensured permanent French control; two months later they landed at Port Sudan to take part in the British campaign against the Italians. The British at first looked down on the Legion as a rag-tag lot but, as always, the legionnaires quickly earned respect and popularity. The 13th was so successful in the Sudan and Eritrea that General de Gaulle pulled it out and added it to the British-Australian-Indian force which was to capture Syria.

The Foreign Legion in Syria was, of course, under Vichy control. The force of three thousand included the 1st Regiment of Cavalry of the Legion, which was on patrol duty in Syria. It soon became apparent that it was to be used against the British forces. An Englishman was serving in this regiment and, as soon as he heard the news, he deserted and made a long and dangerous journey to Cairo, hoping to join up with the British forces. When he arrived, the first person he ran into was his platoon commander of the previous year, on leave from the 13th Demi-Brigade. He was an *adjudant-chef* of German origin who had opted to fight for the Free Legion. 'Where are you off to?' he asked.

The Englishman told him. 'Oh no, you don't,' the sergeant-major said. 'I'll have no desertions on my conscience. You're coming along with me.'

He cut short his leave, took the Englishman in tow and returned with him to the 13th Demi-Brigade, where the Englishman remained for the duration of the war.[60]

Most military men expected that the Vichy forces in Syria would put up a token resistance, but it was firm and fierce and, ironically, the main resistance came from the 6th (Vichy) Foreign Legion Infantry Regiment. Legion fought Legion, and bloodily, but sometimes odd things happened. A 6th Regiment post spotted a 13th Demi-Brigade patrol and ambushed it; the 6th Regiment officer turned out his guard, presented arms to the captured officer and said, 'You are the enemy but first you are legionnaires.' Other men of the 6th prevented Senegalese troops from beating up and robbing 13th wounded—yet minutes later opened up with machine-guns on other 13th sub-units. Nearly always both sides gave full military honours to dead legionnaires.

When the Allies occupied Syria it was turned over to the Free French, whose administrators dissolved the 6th Regiment but gave its three thousand legionnaires the choice of being repatriated to Vichy territory or joining the 13th Demi-Brigade. In this way the 13th acquired another one thousand men. About this time Colonel Amilakvari—the Georgian Prince Dmitri—took over the 13th Demi-Brigade. Amilakvari had been with the Legion since 1924 and was efficient and popular. 'We foreigners,' he told his men, 'have only one way to prove to France our gratitude for the welcome they have given us. We can kill her enemies for her.' Morale went up after Dmitri Amilakvari took over.

Meanwhile a Legion detachment, under the brilliant Colonel (later General) Le Clerc, made an incredible march up the Congo and Ubangi Rivers—2,000 kilometres of it—to capture Fort Lamy on Lake Chad. Without Fort Lamy Allied planes could not fly the width of Africa, with all that this meant in communication, supply and liaison. From Fort Lamy Le Clerc led his 'force' towards the Italian forts, deep in the Sahara, capturing one after the other, until on 1st March 1941 they took Kufra, 500 miles from the Mediterranean.

The Free French troops, including Le Clerc's men, joined the British Eighth Army in the Western Desert, and in February 1942 were posted at Bir Hakeim, a desert defensive box at the southernmost point of the British line. Attacked on 27th May 1942, first by Italian armour and then by German armour supported by Stuka dive-bombers, the legionnaires and other Free French troops held out until 2nd June. With water, food and ammunition low, the Legion was ordered to break out on the night of 10th–11th June. Their evacuation was so successful that next morning the German guns bombarded an empty position; the Legion had got clean away, although their casualties had been heavy during the siege.

One of the Legion's most interesting members ran the gauntlet out of Bir Hakeim, though strictly speaking she was not a legionnaire.

She—Susan Travers—had joined the 13th in England, in 1940, as an ambulance driver. She accompanied the legionnaires throughout the 13th's campaigns and was General Koenig's jeep driver during the Legion break-out through the German minefield at Bir Hakeim. She remained with the Legion, still as a driver, to serve in Indo-China. Miss Travers was an exception. The notion that somehow women have slipped through the medical inspection and have served as legionnaires is another fantasy.

Many British accounts of the battle of Alamein, October 1942, omit any reference to the Legion, but at the height of the battle the 13th Demi-Brigade was sent to take El Himeimat escarpment. The legionnaires cleared the ridge and were then swept off it by a German counter-attack. Amilakvari led the 13th back to the ridge and they took and held it, but Amilakvari was blown to pieces by a mortar shell.

Legion loyalties, inevitably, were strained. When the Americans and British landed in North Africa behind the Germans in Libya it was natural that German legionnaires should feel an emotional pull towards Rommel; some plotted to hold the Mareth Line for him, though this came to nothing. In Morocco the great mass of Spanish legionnaires plotted to overthrow their German *sous-officiers* should they resist the Allies and the *sous-officiers* took the hint.

The 13th Demi-Brigade stayed with the 8th Army until it reached Tunisia, where it became involved in heavy fighting at Jebel Garci on the southern flank of the Mareth Line. Its opponents were men of the formidable German 90th Light Division, but they were pushed out. By now the 13th Demi-Brigade was reduced to 1,200 all ranks, and at the end of the North African campaign total Legion strength in the region was well below ten thousand. This meant a drastic reorganization centred around the 13th Demi-Brigade which, in April 1944, was sent to Italy to join the British Fifth Army.

After much contact with the slowly withdrawing Germans, the brigade was ordered to capture an enemy blocking position at Radicorfani—a superb natural defensive position atop an escarpment. In a battle that has received little attention the legionnaires moved against the Germans across a line of heights. Unable to advance by normal methods they adopted well-tried Legion tactics of small detachments making their own way up the escarpment to bomb the Germans out.

Several Legion units were present in France after the Allied invasion of Europe, but the 13th Demi-Brigade was the first to set foot in France since 1940; they landed at Cavalaire, Provence, on 6th

August 1944. The legionnaires took the leading part in driving the Germans from Lyons and several units were prominent in the hard-thrust campaign towards Alsace and the Rhine. At some cost they took several Rhine bridges intact. The last action for the 13th Demi-Brigade was the battle for Colmar, 2nd February 1945; after this action the Brigade had fewer than one thousand men. Other Legion units had also lost heavily, particularly the RMLE which, street by street, took Lauterbourg, near Stuttgart.

The Legion was considered more proficient than most Allied troops in clearing out pockets of resistance, though sometimes these mopping-up jobs turned into battles, as did the action at Friedrichshafen. They pushed through to the Danube on 24th April, and on 7th May, the date of the ceasefire, legionnaires were in the Arlberg Pass, Austria, in Stuttgart, Coblenz and Baden-Baden, Germany. The 13th was granted the unique right to wear on its badge the Cross of Lorraine because it alone had fought with De Gaulle from the beginning. The Legion had earned whatever glory was accorded it. It had lost 118 officers, 821 *sous-officiers* and 8,076 men killed. This was more than twice the Legion deaths of World War I.

But there was another privilege the old hands, wherever they were, regarded more highly than the right to wear the Cross of Lorraine. 'Now,' they said, 'we can go home.'

They meant Sidi Bel-Abbes.

Chapter 15

New Legionnaires—New Enemies

'The Foreign Legion was brilliant at two things—killing and dying well, both of which the legionnaires did frequently and with *éclat*.' Legionnaire Sergeant Henry Ainley, *In Order to Die*.

Those legionnaires who had spent the war years in Indo-China hardly knew where home was. Theirs was a strange war and they felt themselves forgotten by the world. One of the oddest anomalies of World War II was that after July 1941 when the Japanese invaded southern Indo-China—an act condoned by the Vichy Government —France remained nominally in administrative control of the area. The Japanese left all internal matters to the French, whose five thousand troops—nearly all legionnaires—were permitted to retain their arms and to have 'complete freedom of action'.

It suited the Japanese to have the French police the country while they got on with their war against the Americans, British and Australians. The Japanese had an overwhelming superiority, but were careful not to provoke the Legion, although 'freedom of action' meant remaining static in its bases at Tuyen Quang, Dap Cau and Ventri.

Many legionnaires were induced by the Chinese to desert. They were bored, frustrated by lack of action, anxious in some cases for news from home and eager in many cases for the sexual adventures the Chinese promised them. Desertion seemed attractive. The Legion shrank further as men finished their time of contract, although many stayed with the Legion since they had nowhere else to go. By the beginning of 1945 the French garrison was down to less than three thousand. Then on 9th March 1945 the Japanese presented an unexpected ultimatum: the Legion units must lay down their arms and be interned; from now on Japan would directly control all Indo-China. The Legion refused and skirmishes followed. Legionnaires captured in outposts were treated as barbarically as any other troops taken prisoner by the Japanese.

126

The Legion officers acted quickly. On the same night as the ultimatum, orders went out for all units to merge, and on 11th March the Legion began a fighting retreat to sanctuary in Yunnan, China. They had 500 miles of tortuous country to cross, a land of mountains, jungle and innumerable rivers. The Japanese ambushed the columns several times, but on every occasion the legionnaires charged through. The Legion reached the Yunnan frontier in fifty-two days—a remarkable 'march or die' performance. After another 200 miles they came to their first road, made camp, and here the Chinese let them remain for the moment. The Legion held itself ready, if necessary, for another Camerone.

But within months the Japanese, beaten back all over the vast South Pacific arena, withdrew from Indo-China. There was now a vacuum. The Viet Minh nationalists and their leader, Ho Chi Minh, set up administrative centres in Tonkin, Amman and Cochin-China; these three countries became, together, Vietnam. The Viet Minh did not believe that the French would return, and at first it seemed they would not do so, but the Potsdam Conference declared that northern Indo-China should be occupied by Nationalist China for the time being and that Britain should occupy the southern half. The British were happy to hand over the chaotic situation to the French, who returned to Hanoi on 6th March 1946. The Viet Minh was astounded and angry. Meanwhile the three thousand men of the Legion who had been in Yunnan marched back to their posts, most of them to be repatriated to Algeria. To the Viet Minh this seemed a good sign—but then three new Legion regiments appeared from North Africa.

The legionnaires who were arrving in Indo-China were a mixed bag. The Legion had a strong French element, still posing as Belgian or Swiss. They were idealists—with the wrong ideals, according to their countrymen. They had volunteered to serve with Marshal Pétain's (Vichy) Legion of French Volunteers with the Germans and against the Russians on the Eastern Front. There was a sprinkling of ardent monarchists who had hoped France would cease to be a republic after the war. German SS and French SS men found their way into the Legion, provided French Intelligence and Resistance investigators were convinced they had not taken part in Nazi atrocities.

The Legion recovered itself after the war more rapidly than any other military formation; enmities, frustrations and long-penned hatreds did not need to be exercised here. Men of many nationalities were joining, usually those who had been so unsettled by the war that they could not settle into a normal peace-time life. Some had held commissions. At one time, on an NCOs' course at Saida, twelve of the sixty men had been officers in various European armies, one a colonel in the Wehrmacht. The quality of the *sous-officiers* was so good that many officers almost gave up attending parades and left them to their sergeants. The *sous-officiers* were Olympian-like creatures and were probably more of an *élite* group at this time than in any other period of Legion history. They tended to forget nationality among themselves; it was unpardonable to ask a colleague his nationality and it was bad form to speak any language other than French in the mess. At Sidi Bel-Abbes in 1946 the *sergent-chef* was a German, highly respected by the French *sous-officiers*.

Perhaps the most distinguished legionnaire of the period was Giuseppe Bottai, known in the Legion as Sergeant Battaglia, one-time Minister of Education in Mussolini's Cabinet. He had helped overthrow Mussolini in July 1943, and was then hunted by the Germans but slipped out to join the Legion. The Legion owes him much because his hobby was a study of it; he was one of the very few legionnaires to seek to understand Legion background and psychology.

Englishmen were enlisting, but with unhappy experience of so many English deserters in the past the Legion recruiting officers always gave an English applicant time to reconsider his decision. Colin John was sent for by a captain recruiting officer who politely asked him to sit down. 'I have sent for you so as to give you a last chance to withdraw. Consider a little . . .' and he painted a terrifying picture of life in the Legion, its toughness and its dangers. 'You are going to sign a contract for five years . . . even with your capabilities, you will only arrive, with luck, at the rank of adjutant. In exercising the most strict economy, you might be able to save two or three hundred thousand francs. Is that really what you want?' It was, and John signed his contract—under the name of Smith.

John saw camaraderie at its best during his early days in the Legion. He had fallen ill and could not accompany abroad the detachment of which he was a member. That afternoon he heard subdued whispering and scuffling in the corridor of the hospital and an attendant said, 'All right then, but only five minutes and don't let the doctor see you.' And in came his comrades, including men whose names he did not know. They brought with them a sackful of oranges and two packets of cigarettes—rich spoil from penniless men he had known less than four days. Awkwardly they stood about, wishing him good luck and urging him to get well quickly, before the orderly pushed them out.

With equipment still short after the war Legionnaires were given makeshift uniforms. John's first outfit consisted of a forage cap three sizes too big, a khaki shirt torn down the back, tattered underclothing, a pair of American Army trousers and a 1914 British Army tunic complete with the buttons of the Queen's Royal West Surrey Regiment. He had a *musette* (knapsack) containing a mess-tin, a 'housewife' with neither needle nor cotton and a towel marked 'British Red Cross'.

But before long the legionnaire on parade was as colourful as any soldier in the world—very martial in his white kepi, leather equipment, the blue cummerbund, red-fringed epaulettes, anklets and green tie. Like so much else in the Legion the tie was an opportunist addition to the legionnaire's uniform, for until World War II legionnaires had worn a rather tight stock. In 1945 the French Army Supply Department found it had a large store of green ties, and as nobody else wanted them they were offered to the Legion, which at once adopted the ties as its own.

The men who were arriving in Indo-China in tropical gear as the first units of the post-war Legion, and those which followed, could not then have known that the Legion would be used to spearhead nearly all French offensives, to hold untenable positions and to retrieve the day when others had lost it. They were the first of a Legion force which would reach a strength of sixty-five thousand—a record figure. And for the first time in its history the Legion was developing a political attitude—anti-Communist.

Ho Chi Minh prepared for a long guerrilla war. Arms and ammunition were smuggled in, training camps were established, agents probed into every corner of Indo-China. In three months' guerrilla fighting in southern Amman one Legion battalion lost 235 men; the French knew then that resistance would be extreme. Decisions made in Paris produced a recruiting boom for the Legion, and at Sidi Bel-Abbes, half a world away, thousands of legionnaires were trained for fighting a new enemy in a terrain few of them had yet experienced.

General Giap, Ho Chi Minh's military chief, tried an all-out assault on the French in the Red River Delta, but it was disastrous; Viet Minh casualties were heavy and the French were virtually unscathed. But the Legion lost some good men in those early days. One was Lietenant-Colonel de Sairigne who had spent the whole war in the 13th Demi-Brigade. In 1946, at thirty-three, he was the youngest corps commander in Legion history. He was killed on 1st March 1948. One of his daughters was born after his death and the Legion became her godfather.

129

In compensation, good men also arrived. In 1948 there was a Communist coup d'état in Czechoslovakia, and Karel Hora, now with a wife and child, smuggled his family out to Paris and returned to Sidi Bel-Abbes, from where he was sent, as a major, to command the post at Dinh Bang.

After the failure of fixed-position warfare Giap relied on hit-and-run tactics. The Legion, losing many men in ambushes on jungle trails, resorted to proven tactics in North Africa, by building chains of small concrete forts along strategic routes and stronger defensive posts around the towns. But fighting became more frequent and movement more dangerous. In April 1947 Giap concentrated all his trained guerrillas for an attack on the vital French post of Bac Kan, but to take this he must first capture the defended village of Phu Tong Hoa, held by only 104 legionnaires whose heaviest weapons were two light machine-guns and whose main defences were four palisaded and sandbagged corner bastions.

Giap probably used 1,500 men and ten heavy mortars in this assualt. The attack began on the night of 25th July, and in misty darkness waves of Viet Minh overran three of the bastions. Within minutes the Legion counter-attacked from the fourth post and re-captured one of the lost posts. In a further hour of fierce fighting the legionnaires took another post. With all officers out of action the *sous-officiers* put snipers to work picking off the Viet Minh in the final post, which the enemy then abandoned. After a further hour's fighting Giap's men disappeared into the jungle. At dawn next day the Legion counted 40 enemy dead; they had lost 23 legionnaires killed and 33 wounded. The battalion commander force-marched a relief column to Phu Tong Hoa, where the senior *sous-officier* received his colonel with a ceremonial guard in full-dress uniform.

A gallant young officer, Lieutenant Alain de Woillement, was killed in December 1948. He had been engaged to an American girl, member of an American military family. US officers who had known Woillement and his fiancée had a bronze cross made with this inscription: 'I rose from the chill ground and folded my soldier well in his blanket, and buried him where he fell.' The cross was sent to Sidi Bel-Abbes for the museum.

But not all legionnaires in Indo-China were heroes. Viet Minh agents worked at inducing legionnaires to desert, and during the nine years of war to 1954 at least two thousand legionnaires went over, by French official admission. The true figure was probably much higher. At this time the Viet Minh treated Legion deserters very well, as they did most of their prisoners, and many were sent home to

Europe via Red China. The Legion believes that about three hundred deserters actively helped the Viet Minh. One, Shroeder, an Austrian ex-captain, became a kind of Otto Klems. Taken to Ho Chi Minh, he married one of the great man's nieces, assumed the name of Ho Chi Long and among other duties was said to be training a 'Silver Legion' of Legion deserters. This *élite* unit was to fight as comrades of the Viet Minh, but Shroeder had recruiting problems and no French force ever came up against the Silver Legion.

By 1950 Giap had built up his strength enormously, largely with help from Communist China, and he now had regular infantry units as well as guerrillas. To clear the French from Tonkin his immediate aim was to knock them from the Kao Bang Ridge and thus back to the line of the Red River. The point for attack was Dong Khe, which the Viet Minh shelled heavily on 16th September 1950 before sending in six battalions of infantry the following morning. As at Phu Tong Hoa, the Legion lost three corner bastions, but this time there was no retaking them, though one did change hands eight times in twenty-four hours. By the end of the day the legionnaires were crowded into one defensive post, with 40 dead and 100 wounded. Under incendiary-bomb attack, the survivors formed into a wedge and bayonet-charged their way through the surrounding Viet Minh. Yet another Cameroné.

That year, 1950, the Legion was upgraded by a decree which created the *Groupement de la Légion Étrangère*; this made the Legion an independent corps within the French Army and gave it status similar to that of the US Marine Corps. It was controlled—and still is—by the Inspection Technique de la Légion Étrangère in Paris, an inspectorate commanded by a general with a small staff. But the defeats at Phu Tong Hoa and other places sapped French morale, and until Marshal Lattre de Tassigny assumed command they were too defensively minded. Marshal de Tassigny was a commander the legionnaires understood and he trusted them; in January 1951 a patrol of the 13th Demi-Brigade surprised a guerrilla band and killed more than two hundred of them. The Legion now had its paratroops and several detachments were dropped for patrol and reconnaissance work.

Some young legionnaires were rapidly building up spectacular reputations after the higher morale injected into the French forces by Marshal de Tassigny. Legionnaire Nielsen, aged twenty-three, after only two years in Indo-China had won the Croix de Guerre nine times, the Médaille Militaire and had been promoted *sergent* in the field. Despite having had an arm smashed by an explosive bullet he made spectacular one-man raids against the Viet and had shot down more of them than anyone in the battalion. And he wanted still more—too much. He was killed in an ambush.

The Legion was becoming a more integrated part of the French Army than ever before simply because various French units, unable to find the specialists they needed in their own ranks, sought them from the Legion. The Legion was also diversifying its role, so that it had several motor transport units, river-boat patrols for transport and fighting and an air supply unit. A Legion detachment operated the armoured trains—a sought-after job.

Indo-China sickened many legionnaires because they saw the civilian population as degenerate and immoral. For Colin John the women of Saigon came in only two classes—those who worked and those who whored. The work was tough—stone-breaking, roadmending, bricklaying. To have a baby a woman took off perhaps two days. The others, even if they had a large family, 'went out and whored, while papa sat at home and smoked his pipe of opium'.[61]

Rape was commonplace, notably committed by the Latins and Slavs. It was abhorred by the Germans and Nordic men. Legionnaire Henry Ainley, helping to search a village, saw an Armenian *sergent-chef* grab a girl, violently rip open her jacket and tear down her trousers. As he pulled her to him, and began to fumble with her breasts and buttocks, Ainley pulled him away from her. This saved the girl, but Ainley waited for the severe punishment he could expect for attacking a superior. The *sergent-chef* laughed and told the Englishman he would get used to it. 'In a cowardly way I was relieved,' Ainley confessed. 'I did not feel up to fighting a whole army on the question of well-established traditional sports.'[62]

Even when innocent, the Legion got the blame for everything, largely because of the ill-founded but persistent belief that it was full of ex-SS men and war criminals. Without doubt some such men were in its ranks, but because they were men who could least afford investigation they were generally the best behaved.

However well the Legion fought, it was always hampered by its baggage. A convoy of trucks was needed to carry the equipment of a mere battalion—six hundred men. Each man had several trunks for his kit, his loot and his mementoes; then there were dogs, cats, parrots and congayes. The congayes always accompanied their men; they were socially superior to the women of the mobile brothels and travelled separately from them. Orders prohibiting the congayes from following the Legion companies were never obeyed and many were killed by enemy fire.

Obviously not every legionnaire felt that he would be lost if a congaye gave him her yellow breasts with black nipples, for a common saying was,

Petite Annama, petite Annamite,
Elle avait sur sa poitrine
Deux jolies petites mandarines.

No doubt the Annamite girls' breasts could be likened to little oranges, but some legionnaires found to their exasperation that these girls wanted to put on paper legal contracts about 'even the most natural acts of life'.

If the legionnaires thought that in leaving North Africa they would put road-making behind them they were to be disillusioned. To make one particular road a battalion was divided into two, the groups were placed 200 miles apart and ordered to work towards each other. Since they were following an elephant track as the basis of a route they had to cut nearly 150 miles of a road 15 yards wide. The work consisted of felling trees, clearing undergrowth and building bridges over innumerable mountain streams which crossed the track every few hundred yards. French Army engineers, being specialists, were supposed to make the bridges, but the legionnaires, not being specialists, made them faster and better. The *sous-officier* in charge of a bridging party would name his creation after a famous bridge in his homeland. The road went on at about a mile a day.

During 1953–4, with warfare incessant, the Legion had swollen to several times its normal size and there were not nearly enough officers of the right type. The French Army made the mistake of posting to the Legion officers from more conventional units, men without the skill of their *sous-officiers*, and unable to win their respect. Many of these officers were in Indo-China for one reason only—to make money, for at that time French troops were even more highly paid than American troops. There were officers who could not read a jungle map and others who wore their kepis rather than the customary bush hat, and were therefore easy targets for Viet Minh snipers. There were even officers who ordered that ammunition should be abandoned to the enemy, though the *sous-officiers* rarely obeyed these orders.

No amount of Legion versatility could stem the encroachment of Giap's troops. In April 1953 Giap pulled off a great coup: he invaded Laos, waited until the monsoon broke and then returned to northern Tonkin with the valuable opium crop. The French took this as an affront to pride and professionalism. They decided to establish a major strong-point at the junction of three main tracks in northern Tonkin—the idea being to prevent a repeat performance by the audacious Giap.

The place chosen for this 'centre of resistance', as command termed it, was the village of Dien Bien Phu.

Chapter 16

Sacrifice at Dien Bien Phu

'The legionnaire is not the protagonist of a cause. He is not essentially a soldier performing his duty. He is an individual true to himself. In this light, the confusion and cruelty of the Indo-China War are irrelevant.' Adrian Liddell Hart, *Strange Company*.

The battle of Dien Bien Phu, Indo-China (now in North Vietnam) in the spring of 1954 was one of the greatest military disasters suffered by French arms, but for the Foreign Legion it has practically the same glory as Camerone. The Legion, with much justification, will accept none of the stigma of ineptitude and sheer stupidity which led to the disaster.

As a French bastion, Dien Bien Phu was the brainchild of one French commander in Indo-China, Lieutenant-General Raoul Salan, and the creation of his successor, General Henri Navarre. Really it was nothing more than a village—one of many in the area—but it became a series of large camps, mutually supporting, well sited and dug in and heavily wired and mined. It looked formidable, and as a base and, assuming that the Viet Minh were frightened by it and kept clear, it *was* formidable. But a glance at a map, let alone observation on the spot, showed that it could be terribly vulnerable. Dien Bien Phu was a French island surrounded by vast areas of enemy-held jungle and nothing could get in or out except by air. The place was also a bowl surrounded by low wooded hills, which General Giap was quick to exploit. He massed four divisions of regular troops in these foliage-matted hills and as early as 11th January 1954 he had encircled the French position.

Arrogant and vain, French military and political leaders had only contempt for the Asian enemy, even after years of finding him a dangerous foe. General Navarre believed, on the basis of classic Western military practice, that he could inflict a stunning defeat on the Viet Minh, in the unlikely event that they should seek a static battle. Navarre rather hoped that Giap would give battle, but if he

135

did not, no matter; Giap could make no major move in Indo-China without being forced to take the powerful Dien Bien Phu base into account. It meant, as Navarre saw it, that the French held a strong initiative.

Navarre also believed, partly on the basis of advice from his Intelligence advisers, that Giap lacked the logistic capacity to concentrate enough troops to overwhelm the garrison. The French artillery and air power would pulverize any artillery the Viet Minh tried to emplace on the heights. His big guns, tanks and machine-guns would decimate the Viet Minh infantry battalions once they descended into the valley itself. He counted on being able to keep the two valley airfields open. And, as if all this were not enough to smash the elusive Viet Minh, Dien Bien Phu was garrisoned by the best Foreign Legion and parachute battalions. Legion paras had secured the place in November 1953, and by April 1954 seven of the twelve battalions in garrison were Legion.

But Navarre and his staff had grossly underestimated the skill and resource of the enemy. The general refused to believe Intelligence reports from his subordinate in Hanoi, Major-General René Cogny, that the Viet Minh were concentrating four divisions on Dien Bien Phu; in fact Navarre called this idea a 'Utopian project'. Other lower-ranking French officers tried to warn Navarre of the debacle in the making, but they were told to keep quiet and obey orders. Navarre was simply following the attitude of his predecessor in Indo-China, Lieutenant-General Salan, who regarded General Giap as 'a non-commissioned officer learning to handle regiments'. Navarre made no attempt to understand Giap, but Giap knew all about General Navarre.

Even the Viet Minh encirclement of Dien Bien Phu did not worry Navarre; he had mastery of the air. But then he found that his air-craft were little use. The Viet Minh were concealed by the dense foliage and napalm strafing and saturation bombing had little effect. More dangerously the French had overlooked Viet Minh possession of several heavy guns and anti-aircraft weapons. French air losses were considerable.

But Navarre and others still had so much blind faith in the impregnability of Dien Bien Phu that even the prostitutes were still there—some from the Lai Chau brothel and others brought from Hanoi to amuse the legionnaires in the main centre.

Legion commanders, holding key posts in the Dien Bien Phu complex, were not so confident as their superiors. They were par-ticularly concerned about the limits of visibility for fields of fire. On the night of 12th March the Viet Minh pulled off an exploit that must have worried everybody who heard of it. A commando group got through to Dien Bien Phu airfield, sabotaged the landing strip by letting off explosive charges under the grids and left leaflets in the vicinity. On some, written in French and German, was the warning, 'Dien Bien Phu will be your grave'. On others a crude caricature showed Navarre's hand pushing French soldiers towards a line of daggers.

The principal Legion posts were Isabelle (a battalion of the 3rd Regiment); Beatrice (a battalion of the 13th Demi-Brigade); Hugette (a battalion of the 2nd Regiment); Lalaine or Eliane (a battalion of the 3rd Regiment); Claudine (a battalion of the 13th Demi-Brigade); and the northern strongpoint, Gabrielle. They were roughly in an oval shape around the airfield, on the edge of which Legion HQ had its post.

Giap had tightened the ring then opened up with concentrated artillery barrages. Heavy and accurate, they startled the French. Among the casualties were the CO of the Legion's 13th Demi-Brigade, Lieutenant-Colonel Gaucher, and several legionnaires. The main attack came on 13th March, when waves of Viet Minh infantry attacked Beatrice, where so many enemy dead draped the defensive wire that they masked the fire of the legionnaires. That night the Legion battalion lost its CO, Major Pegeaux, and six other officers killed and had four hundred casualties in all; Beatrice was swamped by screaming waves of Viet Minh troops and lost.

The sudden fall of Beatrice, the absence of any reaction on the part of the commander, Colonel de Castries, and Gaucher's death were deeply damaging to the garrison's morale. Even in the midst of battle Sergeant Sammarco put a ceremonial guard of four legionnaires over his colonel's grave. Soon, he thought, the Legion in other posts would exact vengeance for this death. Beatrice had been taken by surprise; such a thing would not happen elsewhere.

Enemy artillery pounded French positions mercilessly. Colonel Proth, the French artillery commander, once so confident that he had told Army Command that he needed no more guns, felt so bitterly ashamed of the inability of his artillery to inflict any damage on the Viet Minh that he committed suicide with a grenade on 14th March.

At Gabrielle and Isabelle the Legion held off violent attacks, and one dawn, in an unofficial truce—a rare occurrence in Indo-China —the Legion and Viet Minh recovered their dead and wounded. After much more artillery fire the Viet Minh attacked Lalaine, where positions many times changed hands.

Helplessly exposed, Dien Bien Phu became an extraordinary place, with all the defenders below ground during daylight hours, for the

137

Viet Minh had driven many trenches and tunnels towards the defences and could easily pick off the defenders. At night the legionnaires raided these trenches and hundreds of bloody patrol actions took place. Giap's men took a corner of the airfield and, though French helicopter pilots made some gallant flights to take out wounded, Viet Minh anti-aircraft guns soon stopped them.

With the Legion tenaciously holding their remaining positions, Giap stopped the costly frontal assaults and ordered steady encroachment by sapping, thus forcing the French into an ever-shrinking perimeter. About six hundred legionnaires, none trained as paratroops, dropped in on the night of 9th–10th April to stiffen the defence, but these reinforcements were wasted.

The anniversary of Camerone, 30th April, came around during the siege and, traditionally, the story of the epic was read out to the legionnaires in their bunkers and they had their usual extra ration of wine. The senior surviving Legion officer, Lieutenant-Colonel Lemeunier, gave a party in his command post for de Castries, by now a general, Lieutenant-Colonel Marcel Bigeard, Colonel Langlais and the only French military nurse in the doomed position, Geneviève de Galard-Terraube. Lemeunier, immaculately uniformed and wearing his red kepi, offered his guests red wine. None of his guests were legionnaires, so Lemeunier made Castries and Langlais honorary corporals in the 13th Demi-Brigade and Bigeard and Geneviève privates first class. Two days before Castries had invested Geneviève with the cross of Chevalier of the Legion of Honour and with a Croix de Guerre. The legionnaires of Major Clemencon's 2nd Legion infantry held a ceremony of their own; they cut up the regimental flag, each taking a piece and hiding it. Incredibly, about three-quarters of this flag was later gradually retrieved, and in Sidi Bel-Abbes the museum's curators put the pieces together and framed it. It is almost as important in the mystique of the Legion as Captain Danjou's hand.

With defeat starkly imminent, Captain Capeyron of the 3rd Company, 1st Battalion, burnt his company's flag. Bending over the fire which his legionnaires had hurriedly lit, he saw the last letters of the word *loyalty* embroidered on the silk eaten by the flames when the Viets arrived. A Viet officer shouted 'Hands up!' and when Capeyron did not obey some Viets kicked him in the buttocks. At once the legionnaires broke ranks to intervene and Capeyron said sharply, 'Don't move! It's too late.' But his men would have died there to defend him.

Before the final Viet Minh assault conditions in what remained of the French positions were ghastly. The small medical teams, principally that under Major Paul Grauwin who came in as a replacement on 17th February, somehow coped with thousands of casualties under appalling conditions and with inadequate equipment and supplies.

The Viet Minh's last assault began on 6th May. The French had only a few artillery pieces in action and all ammunition was short. Thousands of Viet Minh came out of the jungle as dusk fell and, regardless of casualties, pressed forward. Legion counter-attacks were gallant but futile. After midnight, with the fall of Lalaine imminent, the legionnaires asked permission to make a break-out. They banded together and struck hard at the encircling Viet Minh, but they went down under the vastly superior numbers of enemy.

By daylight on 7th May only the Legion-held Isabelle and a group at Command HQ remained defiant. After another night's fighting Dien Bien Phu fell, but the legionnaires at Isabelle held on still longer with the pitiful remnants of three legionnaire battalions. The senior officer hailed the battalion commanders in turn, 'We fight on!' After fighting for the rest of the day it became clear that night that rapidly decreasing ammunition supplies meant the end. The colonel gave orders for a break-out at nine-thirty and for strict economy in ammunition until that time. The smoke from Dien Bien Phu was heavy and lurid and acrid as the defenders burnt their stores.

At nine o'clock a legionnaire began to sing:

> Heute wollen wir probier'n
> Einen neuen Marsch marschier'n
> Durch den shoenen Westerwald.
> Ach! Es pfeift, der Wind, so kalt . . .
> (Today we want to try
> To march to a new march
> Through the pretty western forest.
> Alas, the wind blows so cold . .)

The colonel let them sing and when the song was over he asked another legionnaire to start up the *Képi Blanc*

La rue appartient a celui qui y descend.
La rue appartient au drapeau des képis blancs.
Autour gronde la haine. Autour grondent les dogmes qu'on abat.
Foulant la boue sombre vont les képis blancs.

Combien sont tombés au hasard d'un clair matin
De nos camarades qui souriaient au destin?
Nous tomberons sans doute . . .

139

(The street belongs to the one who goes down it.
The street belongs to the flag of the white kepis.
Hate grumbles around us. The dogmas which we bash down grumble.
Tramping through the dark mud go the white kepis.

How many have fallen by chance on a clear morning
Of our comrades who have smiled at destiny?
We shall doubtless fall ...)

Then the colonel led his final four hundred relatively fit men into a bayonet charge as he shouted 'Vive la Légion!' And the four hundred echoed, 'Vive la Légion!' And the Legion lived though the legionnaires died.

During the next several weeks seventy men of the Legion trickled into the French lines—the only survivors of the battle.

On 8th May, when Dien Bien Phu died, legionnaires at posts in North Africa were assembled, and commanding officers read them the communique about the fall of Dien Bien Phu and listed the Legion units which had been destroyed or captured. The ceremony ended with the bugle call 'To the Dead'.

During the siege the French lost 1,500 men killed, and 4,000 wounded, more than half of them legionnaires. Another 9,000 were captured and with the wounded marched away into captivity. Under the peace terms, ignominious for France, most Legion prisoners were exchanged a month later. The legionnaires suffered badly in captivity and 70 per cent needed intensive medical treatment after repatriation.

The Legion units went back to North Africa, leaving behind 314 officers and 10,168 legionnaires killed during the nine-year war. Another 30,000 were wounded, but many of these men stayed on in the Legion, which had yet another date with its strange destiny.

Chapter 17

The Great Shame

'The Legion is a hybrid milieu where a man enters masked to display an astonishing fecundity of initiative and a supreme disdain of death.' Quoted by Howard Swiggett in *March Or Die*.

'Bravery is not enough. Everybody is brave out here. This must be done avec chic et avec goût [with style and with taste]. You are une troupe mystérieuse ["mysterious" with the sense of "illustrious"]'. A Legion officer to his men in Algeria, 1958.

'For their officers legionnaires will do anything asked of them, even the most fantastic things. . . .' Colonel Brothier, CO at Sidi Bel-Abbes, in mitigation of the murders committed by legionnaires who joined the OAS terrorist movement in Algiers after the French Government abandoned Algeria.

In Algeria the general feeling was that the Regular Army and not the Legion should have been used at Dien Bien Phu and that the Legion's principal role was in Africa. This was one way of rationalizing the defeat which had so damaged Legion morale. Those legionnaires already in North Africa, and those who returned there from Indo-China, were burning with a desire for action which would vindicate the jungle defeats.

Of course some were content with what had become a fairly pleasant way of life in Algeria. The Legion became a wealthy 'corporation' and one of the biggest landowners, with many farms supplying meat and vegetables to units in respective districts. Run by pensioned-off and partly disabled legionnaires, many of whom had married and settled down to a rural life, these farms were the best run in Algeria. The Legion even had its own fishing boat—the *Anne-Marie*, after a German song popular in the Legion. Manned by a crew of Baltic fishermen from the Legion it would go out from Agadir on Morocco's Atlantic coast and fish with the Breton trawlers. The Legion dined well in Agadir, probably the best posting in Africa.

The re-enlistment rate was high, for the Legion was about to grant

141

a 52,000-franc bonus for a five-year signing, with a further 12,000 francs for each year of service after this. More than 1 million French people lived in Algeria, officially a department of France, and the Legion was accepted among the populace more than ever before. Algeria seemed a fairly peaceful region, but for ten years Moslem leaders had been building up a strong underground movement which became known as the Algerian National Liberation Front, the FLN. Under the noses of the French the FLN acquired a vast quantity of small arms and explosives and trained many young men as guerrilla fighters and terrorists. The Algerian War broke out on the night of 30th November 1954 when thirty FLN detachments hit French posts throughout Algeria.

The French went on the defensive, trying to gauge the seriousness of the uprising. It was very serious, and within eighteen months the French Army was built up to 250,000, but during that time the FLN had gained a firm psychological hold over the Moslem population, largely by terrorism and atrocity.

Despite the pressure, the Legion sent 1,500 paratroops to take part in the abortive Anglo-French Suez operation of 1956. They behaved efficiently but returned to Algeria embittered by what they considered the political 'stab in the back' which had prevented them from achieving their objective—to recover the Suez Canal seized by the Egyptians. It was a minor wound compared with what was to come. When the doyen of the Legion, Regimental Sergeant-Major Collard, died that year at eighty-six, the more cynical legionnaires said that he simply gave up living so that he would not have to see the way the Legion was being treated. Collard had a total of forty-eight years service and, at the age of seventy, had signed on for his last stint in 1939.

The Algerian conflict was a tragedy for the Legion. For one thing the Legion was pro-Moslem; it had built Algeria's roads and railways; its medical officers had saved many Algerian lives in the Aures Mountains and in Kabylia. It was even teaching Berber children how to read and write. The Legion had no personal quarrel with the Arabs. Yet Legion units were used as fighting patrols, searching by day and night and trying to bring the FLN to battle. They made many contacts but were often ambushed, and in 1956 and 1957 they suffered many casualties. The garrison rose that year to 400,000, but French military policy was vapid and hesitant and the FLN gained in prestige and territory held. Algiers became such a hotbed of terrorism, with twenty incidents a day, that General Massu asked for a paratroop division—mostly legionnaires—to sweep the FLN from the city. This they did with crisp efficiency.

The French task was enormous. They had to control infiltration of men and arms across the long Algerian-Tunisian border, which they largely reduced by a double electric fence. When the FLN turned to Morocco for support the French built an electric fence along that frontier too.

French civilian casualties were high. The Algerian rebels, true to tradition, cut throats with fanatical enthusiasm; most of these victims were French farmers in remote communities, their wives and families, all people who had lived in peace with the Algerians.

Desertion was again a problem and perhaps 1,800 legionnaires used escape routes organized by the FLN, which treated them well and shipped them out of Africa. Only a few stayed to fight for the FLN.

By 1958 the Legion—and, indeed, the entire French Army—needed clarification and reassurance; it was necessary to know just what the French Government was going to do amid the horror of the conflict going on in Algerian cities. Officers and men welcomed de Gaulle's rise to power, and when he visited Sidi Bel-Abbes in July 1958 Colonel Thomas, 1st Legion Infantry, showed him the museum exhibits and the roll of honour of all Legion officers killed for France since 1831. 'Mon general,' Thomas said, 'will all these have died for nothing?'

'Have confidence in me, Thomas,' de Gaulle said.

At the end of the year de Gaulle removed General Salan and appointed General Maurice Challe as C-in-C Algeria. An able strategist, tactician and leader, Challe completely reorganized French strategy and planned to drive the FLN south, using his four hundred helicopters to spot FLN groups for his half million troops.

He formed the Legion and French paratroop units into small fast-moving columns, and within months broke the FLN from an active fighting strength of 100,000 to 15,000 desperate men who fought only to escape when cornered.

The Legion was used for 'tough' jobs. During 1959 the 3rd Regiment killed 462 rebels, took 664 prisoners and captured 12 medium machine-guns and 350 other weapons. That year the 1st Legion Parachute Regiment claimed to have killed 972 rebels for a loss of 42 dead and 97 wounded legionnaires. An armoured unit, the 2nd Cavalry Regiment known as the Dauphin Étrangère, killed 383 rebels. But all this was at great cost, and Legion casualties throughout the Algerian War annually averaged about 1,500 killed and wounded.

Some legionnaires, disguising themselves as rebels, tracked down the redoubtable and sinister Redouane, who had organized the underground supply of arms from Morocco into Algeria. He refused to surrender and was killed in the consequent fight, but the Legion buried him with military honours.

For some time Colonel Marcel Bigeard, not a legionnaire but one of their great supporters and a *type*, had so thoroughly infiltrated the Algiers terrorist organization that he ran it himself, through his men at the top. When he knew all he needed to Bigeard closed in and captured all the leaders. At this time many Algerians were ready to return to the French, if they could be sure that the French intended to stay. Legion officers also wanted to be sure; one was Colonel Karel Hora, now commanding the 3rd Legion Parachute Regiment.

All felt in need of encouragement from the top. It did not come in 1959, though the following year Legion morale got a boost from Edith Piaf, always a Legion supporter, who dedicated to the Legion her hit record, 'Non, je ne regrette rien'. (See Legion Songs, p. 163.)

The French had the war won; the FLN kept alive only by remaining in Tunisia. The French Army at this time was the best since 1914, highly professional and experienced. Convinced that the war was over, in the more remote regions the Legion went back to building roads, to educating children—the civilian teachers had fled. This was one of the areas where lived many of the 8 million Mussulmans, who were grateful for Legion friendship. At night FLN agents would slip in and warn how dangerous it was to collaborate with the French; a man could get his throat cut for such a thing. But the Mussulmans counted on Legion protection.

Despite friction, Algeria was back to normal and the Legion was content enough even though Challe, who had masterminded the miracle, was back in Europe. The commander now was General Massu. In January 1960 de Gaulle recalled Massu to France; this step was disastrous. The Europeans saw it as a move in favour of the FLN, became frightened and flooded into the streets to demonstrate; French police were shot dead by French civilians. Barricades—a peculiarly Gallic symbol of protest—went up in the streets.

Sidi Bel-Abbes felt the shock wave. Colonists and Mussulmans alike were scared; they had co-operated with the Legion because they believed in French promises. Colonel Brothier of the Legion drove through the city, and over a loudspeaker gave more promises. 'I give you my word as an officer that the Legion will not leave Algeria and above all it will not leave Sidi Bel-Abbes, which is our land and our country. Do not panic. I give you my word. . . .'

Regular French troops refused to take action against the insurgent *colons* in Algiers who defied General de Gaulle over the dismissal of General Massu. De Gaulle moved in the Legion and the *colons* surrendered suddenly. They were given the choice of joining the

Legion to fight the FLN or of standing trial for civil insurrection; 420 were accepted for the Legion but were quietly discharged a few months later. Civil war was narrowly averted.

But Brothier and every other French officer slowly began to see what the politicians were doing throughout 1960 and into 1961— selling out. They could not understand it, for the FLN was finished as a fighting force and the Legion and paratroops controlled the Algerian countryside. Many officers resigned, including Colonel Hora because he 'could not lose another part of his honour'. More than 1,200 legionnaires had died in action against the FLN, another good reason for their comrades' anger at the handing over of Algeria to the terrorists.

Some generals were ready for rebellion, notably Salan, Edmond Jouhaud, André Zeller and Paul Gardy, Inspector of the Legion. And Challe. The participation of this Gaullist general in the intrigue shows the intensity of feeling in the French Army. He resigned from the Army to devote all his time to the plot; he believed that the politicians could not see the importance of holding Algeria, and the ease with which it could be held. He was ably supported by several competent colonels, including Dufour of the 1st Legion Parachute Regiment, the Legion's *élite* unit, and the one with the deepest attachments in Algeria.

General de Gaulle, aware of the plotting, replaced Dufour with Guiraud, a man he could count on not to join a revolt, and to prevent his regiment from doing so. But many other officers were committed to the plot, which continued to ferment. The day of disaster was 11th April 1961 when de Gaulle, at a press conference, announced that France was getting out of Algeria; there was a limit, he said, to how much money could be poured into the place. Next day French rioters in Algiers exploded more than a hundred bombs.

Then Colonel Guiraud, de Gaulle's man, went on leave. The plotters acted quickly. General Jouhaud sent a plane to bring Challe and Zeller to Algeria and Salan was ready to move in from Spain. But the generals found that the 1st Parachute Regiment—the key military unit—was commanded in Guiraud's absence by Major Elié Saint Marc, one of those rare officers not merely admired by his men but revered by them. Saint Marc was so tough and courageous, intelligent and honest, that no general other than Challe dared approach him. His regiment might be ripe for mutiny, but if Saint Marc merely shook his head gently they would be immobile. He had that power.

For Challe the whole thing was a matter of conscience and he presented it as such to Saint Marc, who sided with him and was given orders to maintain law and order in Algiers. The revolt broke in the early hours of 22nd April 1961, with Saint Marc's men taking over key installations with superb efficiency; four generals were taken prisoner. In one hour the rebels held the police stations, post office and government bureaus and only one shot had been fired.

But one thing was overlooked—the telephone line to Paris. Army Command in Paris had troops moving in France within an hour—all under General Ollie, a legionnaire who had orders to quell the rebellion. Whatever the emotions in Paris there was no doubting French enthusiasm in Algiers that day. Citizens garlanded Legion jeeps with flowers and girls arrived in droves to hug and kiss the legionnaires on duty in public places.

Not all Legion units followed the 1st Parachute's lead. The 2nd Parachute Regiment in principle joined the revolt, but its commander, Darmuzai, kept the unit static. The 1st Legion Cavalry tried to have it both ways; its officers had agreed to join the revolt, but to avoid having to make a decision took off after some FLN terrorists on the Tunisian frontier. The 13th Demi-Brigade was in emotional turmoil. How did a regiment which wore the Free French Cross of Lorraine on its badge join in a mutiny? Yet most of the officers wanted to. The CO, Colonel Vaillant, paraded all his officers and *sous-officiers.* 'If you want to join the seditious uprising, gentlemen,' he said, 'there is a preliminary step. You will have to get rid of your commanding officer.' The 13th continued its campaigning in the Kabylia Mountains.

Colonel Brothier, in Sidi Bel-Abbes, also torn by conflicting emotions, held his parade in the Legion's cinema. '. . . I cannot understand why they have brought the Legion into politics. It can only end in disaster. And after all our sacrifices. We do not move from here.'

Then Salan flew in from Spain. He was the senior general, but he had none of Challe's forthright honesty. No radical, Challe spoke the truth when he said that neither he nor the others had any political ambitions. And he was right, except for Salan. The French settlers, and especially the extremists of them, knew they could work on Salan as they could not on Challe. The 'Hold Algeria' movement split and from that moment its cause was lost. Begun on Saturday, the revolt ended on Tuesday from lack of support. By dawn next morning the 1st Parachute Battalion was back at Zaralda. Saint Marc was told that the regiment would be broken up and dispersed, but he was to remain in charge until that time; more or less in charge—two gendarmes followed him at all times.

146

On 27th April the bitter, frustrated and perhaps shamefaced legionnaires smashed their barracks and made bonfires of the furniture. Trucks arrived to take them to Sidi Bel-Abbes and Saida. As their wives and many citizens threw flowers into the trucks the men sang Edith Piaf's song. Many of these men did not reach Sidi Bel-Abbes and Saida; they deserted *en route*, not this time to get out of the country but to stay in it as members of the underground army now being formed.

By now 200 of the Legion's 650 officers had been arrested. Less than a week after the revolt Camerone Day came around, but this time there was no celebration, no reading of the epic, no extra wine. And on 14th July, Bastille Day and France's greatest military occasion, the French Foreign Legion, the most decorated formation in the French Army, was not represented in the Paris celebrations; its flag was not even shown.

The rebels, from general to legionnaire, were too busy to be conscious or even aware of this insult; they were forming the Organisation de l'Armée Secrète, the now notorious OAS. They held Algiers and Oran and they were glorified by the French citizens of Algeria. For the first time in nearly a century there was glory in being a deserter from the French Foreign Legion. Captain Danjou and Fernand Maire could never have understood such a thing.

The revolt, though inspired by the best of intentions, ended the life of the Legion in Algeria and undermined French Government confidence in the corps. The veteran legionnaires were morose, bitter and envious. They longed to be back in Indo-China, where the US was now pouring in troops, equipment and money. The thought of Americans among their beloved congayes drove some legionnaires to suicide and many to *cafard*. Many laughed cynically when they heard that the Sultan of Morocco was sending his troops into the Riff to put down Riffian rebellions. Nobody considered his troops brutal and ruthless, although they were infinitely more so than the Legion had ever been.

At one time a rumour flashed through the Legion that the United Nations was about to ask the Legion to police the Congo. It was wishful thinking. The Legion would have been happy to go and to use its 130 years of experience in such matters; its reputation would have been enough to prevent many of the atrocities the UN troops could not check. The delegates of the UN could not seem to understand that in sending the Legion they would not be sending French national troops but efficient professionals who had sworn allegiance only to a flag.

The rebel officers were brought to trial, and Major Saint Marc spoke for a good many of them when he addressed the president of his court of inquiry. 'What I have to say is simple. Since I came of age I have known only bad experiences; the Resistance, the Gestapo, Buchenwald, Indo-China, the Algerian War, Suez and again war in Algeria. In Algeria we were given a simple mission—defeat the adversary, and then get into motion some form of political equality. They made us jacks-of-all-trades. We did everything because nobody else wanted to do it. We put into this task all our faith, all our enthusiasm, all our youth. All we encountered in return was indifference, the incomprehension of many, the insults of others. Many of us lost our lives. And then one day they told us our mission had changed. We could not understand it. They told us we should start thinking about leaving Algeria. We wept. It was a fitting epilogue to fifteen years of breach of trust; we remembered Dien Bien Phu, and the Vietnam villages abandoned to Communists. Of those men and women who clung to us even as we abandoned them. And then General Challe came! We loved and admired him. He saw us. He told us we had to complete our victory, that we had to remain faithful to the promises we had made to the population, that we had to save our honour. . . . Monsieur le President, one can ask a soldier to die—that's his job—but not to lie, not to cheat, not to perjure himself. There is obedience, I know. But this burden of discipline fell heavily on our shoulders. For fifteen years I have seen legionnaires die. They were French, not by the blood of their birth but by the blood they shed for France. It was for them that I chose. . . .'

Saint Marc's eloquence was wasted. He was demoted and given ten years in prison. Challe and Zeller were degraded and given fifteen years. Sentenced to death *in absentia* were Salan, Jouhaud, Gardy, Argoud, Broizat, Gardes, Godard and Lacheroy. Many Legion officers from colonel to lieutenant were punished by suspended sentences.

In the meantime the OAS had gained a strength of about 2,700, including about 150 hard-core legionnaires. The most distinguished Legion recruit was Colonel Dufour, who had missed the rebellion he would have joined. With his comrades impotent in prison, Dufour did what seemed to him the most honourable thing: he went back to Algeria and offered his services *to save a part of France.* But he and the others in their blind frustration and fury brought about a state of terror rare in modern times, a terror worse than that of Ulster. They had a reason for this madness; they hoped to force the French Government to step in as overlord and protector to obviate what would be bloody vengeance should the FLN achieve its

148

victory. The OAS was formidable, for it had the backing of the entire European population, including a million French people.

General de Gaulle destroyed the OAS and the last great legionnaires by forming old comrades of his Free French Army into an unofficial counter-terrorist force which he sent to Algeria with *carteblanche* instructions to kill and destroy. These were the so-called barbouzes, as dedicated to de Gaulle as the disciples were to Christ. In one of the grimmest, most vicious fratricidal conflicts in history the barbouzes gradually gained the upper hand. Generals Salan and Jouhaud were captured without a fight but treated roughly. Now the police, who had been fence-sitting to see which side would win, went on the offensive against the OAS. When Commissaire Gavoury, chief of the Algiers Sûreté was assassinated, the police raided OAS dens and caught the five murderers. They were all legionnaires—three Germans, a Czech and a Hungarian.

The OAS, Legion-led, had a last spectacular victory in March 1962 when a uniformed squad penetrated the central depot of the Oran Army Group and stole 209 bazookas, 38 heavy machine-guns, 3,000 rifles and 7 trucks. But it was too late. Independence was announced in July and Salan, from prison, called on the OAS to lay down their arms and co-operate with the new regime. Salan, like all his colleagues, was under the ingenuous impression that the Moslems really loved the French and that relationships would be amicable. General Gardy of the Legion assumed command and told a journalist: 'For seven years the FLN killed and mutilated innocent women and children. We fought them but the rest of the world condoned the FLN. Now, when the OAS kills, the world calls us murderers. When we have won the Moslems over to our side and re-established French Algeria, I shall retire to water my flowers. Without France, Algeria is nothing.'

It was Colonel Dufour who implemented the order to cease fighting and gave the order *sauve qui peut*. He fled to Spain, and other legionnaires slipped away to their own countries.

The Legion prepared to leave Sidi Bel-Abbes. Everything removable in the barracks was removed; even the great memorial statue was taken apart and crated; The FLN would have blown it up. The Legion left nothing the FLN could flaunt as Legion property, except a single typewriter. Until the last minute a Legion clerk, who could not believe that he was leaving Sidi Bel-Abbes and had gone strangely *cafard*, was typing out a ration order for the next day. In a final check of the barracks the man was found and led to safety. He was the last legionnaire on duty in Algeria.

At sunset on 24th October 1962 the Legion trumpeters sounded

Retreat within the white walls of Sidi Bel-Abbes for the last time. The long lines of legionnaires stood motionless and silent as an officer paid an eloquent tribute to the Legion dead in Algeria. In conclusion he read a poem written by Captain de Borelli many years before after his orderly, Thiebald Streibler, had sacrificed his own life to save his captain:

> And now would the French understand
> That war is tooth for tooth, eye for eye,
> And that the foreigners who are dead
> Have saved them mourning by falling?
>
> ... If you do not know all that is past,
> And if you are not lying dead for nothing,
> If you have not died for a dead cause,
> O my poor friends, do not ask!

The sentiments were bitter enough to meet the mood of the men who heard them.

Chapter 18

Present and Future

'The Legion is a thing apart ... an anachronism, an incredible survival.'
P. C. Wren. (One of the few accurate observations Wren made about the Legion.)

The Legion was unhappy after its 'retreat' from Algeria. Corporately and individually, it was disillusioned, embittered and suffering from a form of *cafard*. Everything seemed hopeless. When it returned to France under a cloud of distrust some important politicians and soldiers favoured its abolition. For one thing, they said, there would be no work for the Legion now that Indo-China and North Africa were lost to France. It was variously described as an impossible luxury, an anachronism and a breeding ground for future mutinies. The legionnaires had to swallow many insults and their morale was at a low ebb.

For how long could the Legion, a fighting force *par excellence*, live on its laurels? Where in a shrinking anti-colonialism world could the Legion march or die? Where could it exercise its *honneur et fidélité*? There could hardly have been one man who did not feel betrayed by General de Gaulle and his supporters. This sense of betrayal was heightened by the obvious fact of history that the Legion's past was essentially involved with lost causes. Yet in Algeria the cause had been won; the FLN enemy had been beaten. This had made no difference. French politicians had defeated the Legion.

The Sidi Bel-Abbes establishment was moved to the pleasant town of Aubagne, near Marseilles, and the great monument to the dead was set up in the centre of the parade ground. For a time some old legionnaires called Aubagne 'the new Sidi'. But most of the Legion was transferred to Corsica, where discontent found expression in drunkenness and slovenliness. For several years many legionnaires were so maladjusted that they walked around the harbours looking for yachts and ships with foreign flags, then they would swim out and

151

beg to be taken away from Corsica. Most Corsicans did not welcome the idea of the Legion on the island and for a time the coastguards took to shooting at legionnaires in the water and killed some of them. A few coastguards were then found dead in mysterious circumstances and that practice ended.

Almost all news was bad at that time. The Legion heard that the Moroccans had even dug up the bones of old Marshal Lyautey and shipped them back to France. Lyautey had made Morocco, but, now, long dead, he was *persona non grata*. Legion graves throughout North Africa were defaced or simply removed. Those legionnaires whose comrades had died in North Africa felt deeply all these affronts.

There were strong rumours that the Legion would be 'sold' to the United States, a wild idea without substantiation. Under French law the Legion cannot be ceded to any other country, though there is nothing to prevent its being a part of a United Nations force. This could result in a minor administrative problem, for legionnaires cannot be compelled to fight against their own country. Such safe-guards have given the Legion a stability.

In the mid 1960s the Legion gradually settled down, especially with the influx of new recruits who were not really affected by the trauma of the recent past. Foreign postings were made. The 13th Demi-Brigade was sent to Djibouti in French Somaliland; the 3rd Infantry to Diego Suarez in Madagascar. For a time small units were dotted in the Sahara in other countries of the still-contracting French empire.

A new policy was formulated and Legion units became combined teams specially formed for specific missions, with priority responsi-bilities in Metropolitan France. Only three of the six Foreign Legion regiments, with a total strength of 7,500 men, are stationed outside Metropolitan France and Corsica. In a radical departure from tradition, overseas tours for legionnaires are limited, from twenty-four to thirty months.

In 1973 one regiment was in Madagascar and the nearby Comoro Islands; another had its headquarters in New Caledonia from where it provided support for the Central Pacific Test Range, where French nuclear weapons are tested. Part of this regiment is in Tahiti—the 'plum' Legion posting. The third foreign station was French Somaliland at the southern end of the Red Sea. From isolated outposts the regiment assigned to this area carried out border patrols and reconnaissance missions—and, of course, built roads.

The 2nd Foreign Legion Parachute Regiment, in 1973, was

attached to the French Army's 11th Airborne Division in Corsica; this unit is equipped and organized as a standard parachute regiment. Several units of the 2nd Paras were sent to Chad, former French territory, in the spring of 1969 in support of the Government under terms of an agreement with France.

The three reconnaissance squadrons of the 1st Foreign Legion Cavalry Regiment are stationed in Metropolitan France. Protection of vital installations and strategic points against airborne or guerrilla attacks is the mobilization duty of this regiment. Capable of performing a wide range of armoured cavalry operations, the 1st Cavalry Regiment has its HQ at Orange, about seventy miles north of Marseilles.

Aubagne might be the heart of the Legion, but Corsica is the body and is likely long to remain so. Climatically and scenically and in ethos it is very different from North Africa. The mountains of Corsica are lush and green, unlike the Aures Mountains of Algeria, harsh, yellow and forbidding. In Bonifacio there is a Rue Danton with African-like cafés and bars, but one needs a wild imagination to create the illusion that this could be Africa. In summer certainly there are hot, dry winds which make the older legionnaires homesick for North Africa, and then they buy Algerian wines such as Mascara to nurse the nostalgia into something stronger. Many of the bars and other places are run by ex-legionnaires, including a travel agency whose manager was a *sous-officier*. Through the glass of his office window he watches the legionnaires strolling in the street and professes to find them weak and soft. 'How can they be otherwise, these boys, when they have no fighting? They are now a tourist attraction. I confess I exploit them as such and I am ashamed.'

At the main training base of Corte there is a Legion prison, complete with watch-towers, but Legion officers call it 'the improvement centre'. Another kind of improvement centre is the Legion brothel, but the legionnaires complain about the ugliness of the bawds who staff it.

The men of the Legion come mainly from the same backgrounds as those who preceded them since 1831. There is one great difference: French nationals are eligible for enlistment without the subterfuge of posing as Belgians or Swiss. Even so, Germans predominate— 25 per cent to the French 20 per cent, and in 1974, 70 per cent of the *sous-officiers* are German or Austrian. The officer structure is a little different. Legion establishment allow for only one foreign colonel and one lieutenant-colonel in the entire Legion; one major to each regiment and one captain to a battalion. They need to be outstanding to compete professionally with the French officers, for

153

the Legion still has the pick of the officer cadets passing out of St Cyr. Some French people consider that a higher proportion of the junior officers should be foreign and that at least six colonels should be non-French. But since the Legion is now much more integrated with the French Army the Army hierarchy would oppose too many senior posts being held by foreigners.

Lack of opportunity for combat has meant that the Legion has few officers of the type of Rollet, Aage, Maire and Pechkoff, but the philosophy of leadership is the same—pride, professionalism, élan and ésprit. In the 1920s young Legion officers were told, 'In the Legion, when you are not quite sure you can do something, give your word of honour to do it. If you *are* sure, make a bet.' There has been little change.

More sophisticated modern training methods have forced the Legion to seek younger men, and recruiting efforts are concentrated on those eighteen to twenty years old. The average age of a Legion recruit in 1973 was twenty-three years before induction. The maximum age on enlistment is forty. The recruit is not even left to choose his own name, but is offered a selection of names and given a new *persona*, right down to a new date and place of birth. All official. In fact the majority of legionnaires retain their real names. After the usual military classification tests the recruit is sent to four months of basic combat training. Specialty training follows, either with the French Army or at civilian adult training centres. The recruit is not assigned to his regiment until after specialty training; thus the traditional isolation of the legionnaire from society has been abandoned.

The Legion's standards of physical fitness, military expertise, discipline, equipment, food, pay and welfare are equal to the best in any army in the world. Many of today's legionnaires enjoy talking of their tough life and the occasional bloody-mindedness of their instructors, but training in the 1970s is no more arduous than, for instance, among British Royal Marine Commandos or the Special Air Service unit. Today the legionnaire spends most of his time in camouflage suit and green beret, and wears the white kepi and fringed epaulettes only for parade occasions or when on guard duty.

The Legion has its supporters, who say that it still functions as a valuable social institution by providing a haven for young men who decide to leave their homes for family, social or political reasons. The Legion itself claims that it provides an environment where many outcasts can recover their sense of identity and find a productive, satisfying role. There has been little change in motives for joining since Legionnaire Jean Martin wrote forty-four years ago, 'One enters the Legion quite often as one enters a monastery, for want of money, want of love, want of honour. . . . One enters for disgust of life, disgust of men or disgust of oneself. . . . One enters in order to disappear, to forget, to be forgotten. . . .'[63]

Nowadays the Legion must be satisfied that a recruit is not a felon or a man accused of serious crimes, but delinquents and minor offenders are accepted as readily as before. Enlistment is for five years, with the option of leaving after four months, and a small pension if the legionnaire re-signs and does fifteen years in all. Since 1937 it has been possible for a commanding officer to discharge a legionnaire of bad character, but the legionnaire would need a really evil character to have himself fired on these grounds. In more recent days a legionnaire is not considered bad enough to be kicked out unless he has been in detention for over two hundred days a year for at least two consecutive years. A man exploiting this rule to get out must be feeling desperate.

Despite its having become a sophisticated force of motorized infantry, airborne troops and light armour, the Legion remains self-reliant, and proud of it. While still at Sidi Bel-Abbes it had set up its own welfare organization, the Service du Moral et des Œuvres de la Légion Étrangère (SMOLE). SMOLE controlled the Legion farms, shops and cottage industries and organized the sale of other Legion products such as pottery, carvings and souvenirs. This money was used to provide extra comforts and amenities. After the Legion left Africa SMOLE continued to deal with pensions, family allowances and convalescent camps. To make 'rectification' less official-looking, SMOLE also took over all matters relating to it. A principal SMOLE function is care of the disabled legionnaires at the Legion's own rehabilitation and convalescent centre—'The Home of Captain Danjou'—in southern France. Perhaps more revolutionary, even before the Legion left Africa and France's other overseas possessions, SMOLE was building Legion cinemas and organizing film shows, though in principle the Legion has always been reluctant to interfere with a legionnaire's free time. It has always been his own affair if he wants to drink, loaf or live it up, but amenities are now more in evidence in Corsica.

As for veneration for the Legion's past, there has been no change. Under the indoctrination process young legionnaires soon become conscious of a special camaraderie; they join in old Legion songs—mostly old German marching tunes—and they take pride in the epic of Camerone. The ashes of the Camerone dead still make their sacred rounds of Legion regiments.

About eighty nationalities have served France in the Foreign

155

Legion, and between Camerone, 1863, and 1973 they gave much blood for France. Precise figures do not exist, but at least 1,000 officers, 4,000 *sous-officiers* and 35,000 men lost their lives. *Très formidable.*

The Legion faces two dangers. One is that it may become a mere relic which continues to exist for no better reason than that it does exist. Since it is now really part of the French Army this danger will probably be averted, but in that very fact lies the second and greater danger. To identify too closely with the French Army would make the Legion nationalist and not internationalist in character; it would no longer be a 'legion of strangers'. To safeguard its uniqueness the Legion must maintain some moral, psychological and even geographical isolation; it must not merge. This is difficult in an age when frontiers are easier to cross, economic integration is increasing and education is levelling out the differences between nationalities and classes.

An officer told me that all Legion officers believe that the Corps has a long life expectancy because the French people have a deep sentiment about 'la vieille Légion'. It is, he said, a symbolic embodiment of French military tradition because it is identified with the wars and campaigns of more than a century and the great years of the French Empire. 'The Legion is living proof that the French can lead and inspire; today's officers are the descendants of those who made France the greatest military power in Europe, often with the help of foreign mercenaries.'

Somehow 'mercenary', mostly used in modern times in a derogatory way, does not seem a fair term for the French Foreign legionnaire. A mercenary fights for money in a cause which is not his own. The legionnaire fights in the twin causes of his own redemption and a tradition much nobler than mere nationalism. No mercenary, the legionnaire.

Legion Songs and Poems

The songs of the French Foreign Legion are nearly all in French or German, though some were written in English. The original language version of each is given here, together with a liberal translation intended to express the sense and sentiment of the songs rather than to present a linguistically correct translation.

CAILLOUX
Ils ont cailloux sur toutes les routes.
Sur toutes les routes'y a des chagrins.
Mais pour guérir le monde à la déroute
Ils ont képis sur tous les chemins,
Ils ont képis sur tous les chemins.

ROCKS
There are rocks on all the roads.
On all the roads there is nothing but pain.
But to cure the world of its ailment
You'll see kepis on all the roads.

Start of *Bingen on the Rhine* by Caroline Norton (1808–77)
A soldier of the Legion lay dying in Algiers.
There was lack of woman's nursing, there was dearth of woman's tears.
But a comrade stood beside him, while his life blood ebbed away.
And bent, with pitying glances, to hear what he might say.
The dying soldier faltered as he took that comrade's hand.
And he said, 'I never more shall see my own, own native land.
Take a message and a token to some distant friends of mine.
For I was born at Bingen—at Bingen on the Rhine.'

UNTITLED
We are the famous Legion
That they talk so much about.
People lock up everything
Whenever we're about.

The French Foreign Legion

We're noted for our pillaging.
The nifty way we steal.
We'd pinch a baby carriage
And the infant for a meal.

As we go marching
And the band begins to play,
You can hear the people shouting,
'Lock all the doors, shut up the shop.
The Legion's here today'.

UNTITLED
In Morocco where the sun is breathing with heat,
Lonely stands a legionnaire,
He stands still on the rocks
And holds tightly his rifle.
He nods his head sadly and thinks
Of his country.

NOUS SOMMES DE LA LÉGION
Nous sommes de la Légion
Si loin de nos pays.
Vers le front nous marcherons.
Pour abattre l'ennemi.
Avec nos armes
Nos coeurs et nos vies
Nous défendrons la France
Contre l'ennemi.

We are of the Legion,
So far from our homes.
To the front we will march
To defeat the enemy.
With our arms,
With our hearts and our lives,
We will defend France
Against her enemies.

LE FANION DE LA LÉGION
On nous appelle les fortes têtes
On a mauvaise réputation.
Mais on s'en fout comme d'une musette.
On est fier d'être à la Légion.

Et ce qu'ignore le vulgaire
C'est que du soldat au colon
Ils ont une âme de mousquetaire
Les Légionnaires.

THE FLAG OF THE LEGION
They call us hardheads,
And we have a dreadful reputation.
But we don't give a fuck,
Because we are proud to belong to the Legion.
And what the idiots forget
Is that from the soldier to the colonist,
They have the soul of a musketeer,
The Legionnaires.

LA LUNE EST CLAIRE
La lune est claire, la ville dort,
J'ai rendezvous avec celle que j'adore.
Mais la Légion s'en va
Oui s'en va.
Part au baroud, baroud.
Jeannine je reviendrai.
Et la mitraille autour de moi
Elle ne respecte pas la loi.
Les légionnaires les plus vaillants
Tombent sou le feu, le feu.
Mais ton amour, Jeannine, m'a protégé.

THE MOON IS BRIGHT
The moon is bright. The town sleeps.
And I have a rendezvous with the girl I adore,
But the Legion is leaving for the fight.
Jeannine, I shall return.
The bullets flying around me
Have no respect for the law.
The bravest Legionnaires are falling under the fire.
But your love, Jeannine, has protected me.

SONG OF THE 1st BATTALION LEGION PARATROOPS
Contre les Viets, contre l'ennemi,
Partout où le devoir fait signe.
Soldats de France, soldats du pays
Nous remonterons vers les lignes.

Malgré le vent, malgré les obus
Sous les rafales ou sous les bombes
Nous avançons vers le même but,
Dédaignant l'appel de la mort.

Against the Viets, against the enemy,
Wherever duty calls us,
Soldiers of France, soldiers of our country,
We mount toward the firing line.
In spite of the wind, in spite of the shells,
Under the fusillade or under the bombs,
We advance towards the same objectives,
Let us disdain the call of death.

THE CHANT OF THE 1st LEGION CAVALRY,
sung in 2/4 time and rich in melancholy
Une colonne de la Légion Étrangère
S'avance dans le bled en Syrie.
La tête de la colonne est formée
Par l'Premier Étranger de Cavalerie.

Les Druses s'avancent à la bataille.
En avant, Légionnaires! à l'ennemi!
Le plus brave au combat—comme toujours,
C'est l'Premier Étranger de Cavalerie

Un Légionnaire tombe frappe d'une balle
'Adieu, mes parents, ma patrie
Toutes mes fautes je les ai expiées
Au Premier Étranger de Cavalerie.'

Sur sa tombe, une simple croix d'élève
Sur laquelle ces seuls mots sont inscrits:
'Il a servi, honnête et fidèle,
Au Premier Étranger de Cavalerie.'

A column of the Légion Étrangère
Advances in the bled of Syria.
The head of the column is formed
By the first Foreign Cavalry.

The Druses advance into battle.
Forward, the Legionnaires, against the enemy!
The bravest in combat—as always—
Is the first Foreign Cavalry.

A Legionnaire falls, hit by a bullet.
'Goodbye my friends, Goodbye my country.
All my faults I now have expiated,
For the first Foreign Cavalry.'

On his grave a simple cross now stands,
On which these sole words you can see:
'He has served, honest and loyal,
The first Foreign Cavalry.'

SONG OF THE 1st LEGION CAVALRY

Wir sind die Legionnaire
Vom ersten Regiment.
Wir brauchen keine Schirme
Wenn heiss die Sonne brent.
Fatma, Fatma, schenke den jungen Legionnairen was ein
Fatma, Fatma, schenke den Jungen was ein.

We are the legionnaires
Of the first regiment.
We don't need any shade
When the sun burns hot.
Fatma, Fatma, fill the glasses of the young legionnaires.
Fatma, Fatma, fill the boys' glasses.

CRAVATE VERTE ET KÉPI BLANC

Cravate verte et képi blanc
Où t'en vas-tu, beau Légionnaire?
Je vais où le baroud m'attend.
C'est mon devoir faire la guerre
Nord ou Sud toujours sur la terre,
Notre drapeau va palpitant.
Tout couvert d'exploits légendaires
La joie au coeur, le rage aux dents,
Sur la voie, tracée par nos pères,
Combats et meurs, dur Légionnaire.
Cravate verte, et képi blanc.

GREEN TIE AND WHITE KEPI

Green tie and white kepi
Where are you going, gay Legionnaire?
I am going where the scrap awaits me.

161

The French Foreign Legion

It is my job to make war,
Everywhere that the enemy awaits me.
North or south, always on the earth
Our banner waves,
Completely covered in legendary exploits.
With joy in our hearts, and teeth set,
Along the road forged by our fathers,
Combat and death, tough Legionnaire.
Green tie and white kepi.

EN AVANT
En avant sous le soleil levant,
Tête en haut et les cheveux aux le vent,
Légionnaire sois fier de ton bataillon,
Le premier de la Légion.

FORWARD
Forward under the rising sun,
Head held high, hair in the wind,
Legionnaire, be true to your battalion,
The best battalion in the Legion.

MARSEILLES
Drueber hin die Wellen spuelen.
Drueber hin die Kiele wuehlen:
Perlenschleier in der Nacht.
Zigarettenaugen gluehen.
Grelle Pfiffe. Junge Brueste
warten auf die Hand des Fremden
auf den Sturm und Sturz der Brandung
auf das Schiff aus fremden Haefen
auf den Neonglanz der Kueste. . . .

Waves wash (their way) over it.
Keels dig (their way) into it;
Veils of pearls in the night.
Glowing eyes of cigarettes.
Shrill whistles. Young breasts
Are waiting for the stranger's hand,
For the rise and fall of breakers
For the ship from foreign ports
For the coast's Neon lights. . . .

ANOTHER SONG OF THE 1st LEGION CAVALRY
Adieu, adieu,
O Bel-Abbès, lieu vénére de nos aïeux,
De tradition nous combattrons pour la gloire du fanion.

Goodbye, goodbye,
O Bel-Abbes, place venerated by our ancestors.
Traditionally we fight for the glory of the flag.

SONG DEDICATED BY EDITH PIAF TO THE
FOREIGN LEGION
Non, je ne regrette rien.
C'est payé . . . balayé . . . oublié.
Je me fous du passé. . . .
Balayés pour toujours;
Je répars à zéro.
Non, je ne regrette rien.

No, I regret nothing.
It has been paid for, swept away, forgotten;
I do not give a fuck for the past . . .
Swept away forever;
I am starting again from scratch.
No, I regret nothing.

A LEGION MARCH
En avant, Légionnaire de l'Afrique,
Dédaigneux de la pluie et du vent,
Batailleur et pourtant pacifique,
En avant Légionnaire, en avant,
En avant . . . En avant!

Forward, legionnaire of Africa,
Disdainful of the rain and the wind,
Aggressive and yet peaceful,
Forward, legionnaire, forward,
Forward . . . forward.

SONG OF THE LEGION PARAS
Sautons ensemble! sautons ensemble!
Légionnaires, nous ne reviendrons pas.
Là-bas, les ennemis t'attendent.
Sois fier, nous allons au combat.

Jump together! Jump together!
Legionnaires, we shan't come back.

Over there, the enemy awaits you.
Be proud, we are going to fight.

OLD LEGION CHANT
Partout où nous sommes passés,
Partout où nous sommes tombés,
Nous avons semé de la gloire.
    Rataplan!

Everywhere we have been,
Everywhere we have fallen,
We have sown glory.
    Rataplan!

SONG OF THE MOUNTED COMPANY (1925)
Ah! les djebels! Ah! les djebels!
Les djebels et les pitons!
Qui c'est qui s'les tape?
Qui c'est qui s'les tape?
C'est la Compagnie Montée.
Oh, Susanna, les djebels et les pitons.
Oh, Susanna! Compagnie Montée!

Ah! The hills. Ah! The hills!
The hills and the peaks!
Who is it who wins them for himself?
Who is it who wins them for himself?
It is the Mounted Company.
Oh, Susanna, the hills and the peaks!
Oh, Susanna! The Mounted Company

SONG OF THE 13th DEMI-BRIGADE
Vive la Légion Étrangère,
Et quand défilent les képis blancs
Ils portent tous tête haute et fière
Et s'élancent dans la fournaise,
Le cœur joyeux, jamais tremblant,
Au son de notre Marseillaise,
Savant combattre, les képis blancs.

Long live the Foreign Legion,
And when the white kepis go by
They all carry their heads proudly,
And hurl themselves forward in the furnace,

164

Their hearts joyful, never trembling,
To the sound of our Marseillaise,
Able to fight, the white kepis.

MUSTAPHA

This 'song', a medley of French, Arabic, Italian and odd words from other tongues, is not composed to mean anything. A general-purpose song, it was sung to bolster flagging spirits and aching muscles, to help the miles pass under feet or wheels. As it was bellowed solely for its wild sounds it is untranslatable, except for the first phrases—
'Darling, I adore you'. FLN terrorists sometimes sang 'Mustapha'.

Chérie je t'aime, chérie je t'adore
Como la salsa di pomodoro
Ya Mustapha, ya Mustapha
Ana Bahabak, ya Mustapha
Sabaa sénine fel Altarine
Delwa'ti guina 'Chez Maxim's'.
Wamma yi-gui ké-fo kéfo
Wamma yi-gui kéfo kéfo.

BY THE GRAVE OF A DEAD COMRADE

Un copain dit au bord d'notre trou
Quelqu' bout d'prière
Deux morceaux d'bois en croix . . . un nom . . .
Qu'importe si c'nom la c'est pas l'bon?
C't'un Légionnaire.

A friend says at the edge of the grave
a bit of a prayer. Two pieces of wood in the form of a
cross . . . a name.
Does it matter if the name is not the right name?
He was a Legionnaire.

EUGÉNIE

(Empress of France)
Eugénie, tears in our eyes,
We have come to say goodbye.
We leave early in the morning,
Under a bright sky
. . . to Mexico
Farewell, fair Eugénie,
. . . for a year.

165

UNTITLED
Pour faire un vrai Légionnaire
Il ne suffit pas de boire un coup
Ça, tout le monde sait le faire.
Faut être aussi premier partout.

To be a real legionnaire
It's not a question of merely drinking one glass
That, everybody can do.
You must also be first everywhere.

UNTITLED
Nous oublions avec nos pienes
La mort qui nous oublié si peu
Nous—La Légion.

We forget with our hardships
Death which so little forgets us,
We, the Legion.

Afterthoughts

'Born to make war, the legionnaire finds in it his reason for living and his diversion. Their masculine youth is filled with drunkenness and combative ardour, but combat, wine and love set them on fire and make them heroic in the face of death.' A letter from a French officer in *Képi Blanc*, 1951.

DREAMING OF PAST LOVES
(though to the legionnaire 'past' meant 'lost')
'Never shall I forget the echo of that night.
At death's threshold, I hope she may come
One last time, cradling me in the silence,
Covering my cold face, from the Saharan gloom. . . .'
From *Képi Blanc*, an issue of 1953.

Some Foreign Legion Words

abstauben: acquiring anything by irregular means
baraka: luck
baroud: a fight
bas-offs: lower ranks
bled: desert, open country
bouzbir: brothel
cabo: corporal
cabo-chef: chief corporal
capain: mate
châpeau: good fellow
chic-type: neatly dressed eccentric
chleuh: the enemy
corvée: fatigue duties
coup-de-bambon: sudden physical and mental collapse for no apparent
  reason
crac or *petto-fuori:* a brave man in battle (literally a loud fart)
crapule: a man who eats or drinks too much
cravate: a boaster
dekorier dich: as for *démerdez-vous*
jus: coffee
mec: neatly dressed legionnaire
pinard: any wine
plute: pack-drill with a 70-lb. pack of sand
prêt: pay day
ravio: anything obtained illegally
Rémalé: Legion Regiment of March
Résé: Legion cavalry
soupe: any food
tôle: regimental prison
type: eccentric legionnaire

References

These are sources referred to by number in the text. Others follow alphabetically.

1 John, Colin (1955). *Nothing to Lose*. Cassell, London.
2 Price, G. Ward (1934). *In Morocco with the Legion*. Jarrolds, London.
3 Perrott-White, A. (1951). *French Legionnaire*. Caxton, Idaho.
4 Pechkoff, Zinovi (1926). *The Bugle Sounds* (preface by André Maurois). Appleton & Co., London.
5 Liddell Hart, Adrian (1953). *Strange Company*. Weidenfeld and Nicolson, London.
6 Martin, Frederic (1912). *Life in the Legion*. Everett & Co., London.
7 Armstrong, ex-Legionnaire James Mackinley ('as told to William J. Elliott') (1936). *Legion of Hell*. Sampson Low, Marston & Co., London.
8 Martin, A. L. *Army & Navy Gazette*, 5th October 1933. Martin was a lieutenant in the Territorial Reserve of officers.
9 Maurois, André (1926). In his preface to Pechkoff's book; *see* note 4.
10 *See* note 4.
11 *See* note 3.
12 Rosen, Erwin (pseudonym, E. Carlé) (1910). *In the Foreign Legion*. Duckworth, London.
13 Manington, George (1907). *A Soldier of the Foreign Legion*. John Murray, London.
14 Loehndorff, Ernst (1931). *Hell in the Foreign Legion*. George Allen & Unwin, London.
15 Doty, Bennett J. (pseudonym Gilbert Clare) (1928). *The Legion of the Damned*. Jonathan Cape, London.
16 Duplesis, E. (1940). *The Cohort of the Damned* ('as told to E. C. Trelawney-Ansell'). Sampson, Low, London.
17 Waterhouse, Francis A. (1930). *Bloodspots on the Sand* ('as told to Roger L. Wimbush'). Sampson, Low, Marston & Co., London.

169

References

18 *See* note 1.
19 *See* note 5.
20 *See* note 14.
21 *See* note 12.
22 *See* note 3.
23 Martin, Jean (1930). *Je Suis un Légionnaire.* Paris.
24 Waterhouse, Francis A. (1939). *Desert Carrion.* Sampson Low, Marston & Co., London.
25 Kanitz, Walter (1956). *The White Kepi: a Casual history of the French Foreign Legion.* Henry Regnery Co., Chicago.
26 *See* note 12.
27 *See* note 1.
28 Stuart, Brian (1939). *Far to Go.* Nimmo, Hay and Mitchell, London.
29 *See* note 12.
30 *See* note 6.
31 *See* note 28.
32 Bocca, Geoffrey (1964). *La Légion!* Thomas Y. Crowell, New York.
33 *See* note 6.
34 *See* note 6.
35 *See* note 13.
36 *See* note 12.
37 Lieutenant Cortier's private journal.
38 *See* note 6.
39 *See* note 6.
40 Housman, Laurence (ed.) (1930). *War Letters of Fallen Englishmen.* Gollancz, London.
41 Seeger, Alan (1917). *Letters and Diary of Alan Seeger.* New York.
42 King, David (1927). *Ten Thousand Shall Fall.* Duffield & Co., New York.
43 Rockwell, Paul (1930). *American Fighters in the Foreign Legion.* Houghton Mifflin, Boston.
44 *See* note 32.
45 Magnus, Maurice (1924). *Memoirs of the Foreign Legion.* Secker, London.
46 *See* note 2.
47 *See* note 17.
48 Aage, Prince (1928). *My Life in the Foreign Legion.* Nash & Grayson, London.
49 Sheean, Vincent (1926). *An American Among the Riffi.* Century Co., New York and London.

50 *See* note 4.
51 *See* note 15.
52 *See* note 2.
53 *See* note 4.
54 *See* note 4.
55 *See* note 2.
56 See note 2.
57 *See* note 28.
58 *See* note 24.
59 *See* note 7.
60 *See* note 1.
61 *See* note 1.
62 Ainley, Henry (1955). *In Order to Die*. Burke, London.
63 *See* note 23.

Bibliography

Aage, Prince (1937). *Fire by Day, Flame by Night, with the Fighting Hermits of the African Desert.* Sampson, Low, Marston & Co., London.

Alexander, Michael (1956). *The Reluctant Legionnaire, an Escapade.* Hart-Davis, London.

Azam, Capt. H. (1951). *La Légion Étrangère—Ses Règles Particulères.* Paris.

Azan, General Paul (1936). *L'Armée d'afrique.* Paris.

Azan, General Paul (1907). *La Légion Étrangère en Espagne.* Paris.

Bauer, Hans E. (1957). *Verkaufte Jahre.* Berlin.

Beauvoir, Roger de (1897). *Légion Étrangère.* Paris.

Blond, Georges (1964). *La Légion Étrangère.* Paris.

Bocca, Geoffrey (1964). *La Légion.* T. Y. Crowell, New York.

Bornert, L. (1954). *Dien Bien Phu: Citadelle de la Gloire.* Paris.

Bottai, Giuseppe (1950). *Legion è il mio Nome.* Milan.

Bowe, John (1918). *Soldier of the Legion.* Chicago.

Brunon, Jean (1963). *Camerone.* Paris.

Chevalier, Jacques (1958). *Nous Algériens.* Paris.

Clark, Michael K. (1959). *Algeria in Turmoil, a History of the Rebellion.* Praeger, New York.

Cooper, Adolphe (1933). *The Man Who Liked Hell.* Jarrolds, London.

Delmayne, Anthony (1958). *Sahara Desert Escape.* Jarrolds, London.

D'Esparbès, Georges (1901). *Les Mystères de la Légion Étrangère* (Ernest Flammarion, Editeur). Paris.

Eliot, Captain George Fielding (April 1928). *Infantry Journal.*

Encounter Magazine (December 1958). 'The General and the Terrorist'.

Erlande, Albert (1917). *En Campagne avec la Légion Étrangère.* Paris.

Fabre-Luce, Alfred (1962). *The Trial of Charles de Gaulle.* Methuen & Company, London.

Fall, Bernard (1961). *Street without Joy: Indo-China at War, 1946–54.* Stackpole, New York.

Fauvet, Jacques and Jean Planchais (1961). *La Fronde des Generaux.* Paris.

Fieffe, Eugene (1854). *Histoire des Troupes Étrangères au Service de France*. Paris.

Fontaine, Pierre (1958). *Abd-el-Krim: Origine de la Rebellion Nord Africaine*. Paris.

Gabrielli, Leon (1953). *Abd-el-Krim et les Evénements du Rif.* Casablanca.

Garrie, Robert (1952). *Bernard de Lattre, un Destin Héroïque*. Paris.

Genet, Edmond Charles Clinton (1918). *War Letters of Edmond Genet*. Charles Scribner's Sons, New York.

Grauwin, Major Paul (1955). *Doctor at Dienbienphu*. Hutchinson, London.

Harris, Ted (1945). *Escape from the Legion*. John Murray, London.

Hasey, Lt John F. (1942). *Yankee Fighter, The Story of an American in the Free French Foreign Legion* ('as told to Joseph F. Dinneen'). Little, Brown & Co., Boston.

Hora, Karel (1961). *Mon Tour du Monde en 80 Baronds*. Paris.

Kelly, Russell A. (1917). *Kelly in the Foreign Legion, Letters*. Mitchell Kennerley, New York.

Képi Blanc, the Foreign Legion's journal; various issues.

La Gorce, Paul-Marie de (1963). *The French Army*. George Braziller, Inc., New York.

La Pénétration Saharienne (1930). Published by French Ministry of War.

La Vérité sur la Légion Étrangére (1953). Paris.

Langlais, Colonel Pierre (1963). *Dien Bien Phu*. Paris.

Laniel, Joseph (1957). *Le Drame Indo-Chinois*. Paris.

Lapie, Captain Pierre (1941). *With the Foreign Legion at Narvik*. John Murray, London.

Lartéguy, Jean-Paul (1961). *The Centurions*. Dutton, New York.

Le Livre d'Or de la Légion Étrangère (1931). Paris.

Le Premier Régiment Étrangère de Cavalerie (1947). Paris.

Lecler, René (1954). *Sahara*. Hanover House, New York.

Letters of Henry Weston Farnsworth of the Foreign Legion (1916). Privately printed, Boston.

Loehndorff, Ernst (1931). *Hell in the Foreign Legion*. Allen and Unwin.

Maire, François Victor Marie (1939). *Souvenirs du Colonel Maire de la Légion Étrangère*. Paris.

Matthews, Tanya (1961). *War in Algeria*. Fordham University Press, New York.

Maurois, André (1931). *Lyautey*. Paris.

Mercer, Charles (1964). *The Foreign Legion*. Holt, Rinehart and Winston.

Bibliography

Military Review, April 1971: 'Whatever Happened to the Foreign Legion?'

Morlae, Edward (1916). *A Soldier of the Legion*. Houghton Mifflin Co., Boston.

O'Ballance, Edgar (1961). *The Foreign Legion*. Faber, London.

O'Reilly, Tiger (1930). *The Tiger of the Legion, Being the Life Story of 'Tiger' O'Reilly* ('as told to William J. Elliott'). Greenberg, New York.

Philips, John (1959). *Odd World*. Simon & Schuster, New York.

Poirier, Jules (1895). *Compagne du Dahomey*. Paris.

Price, G. Ward (1934). *In Morocco with the Legion*. Jarrolds, London.

Raulet, André (1934). *Legion Alles*. Berlin.

Renald, Jean (1955). *L'Enfer de Dien Bien Phu*. Paris.

Reybaz, G. Jean (1932). *Le Ier Mystérieux, Souvenirs de Guerre d'un Légionnaire Suisse*. Paris.

Sablotny, Richard (1940). *Légionnaire in Morocco*. Los Angeles.

Servan-Schreiber, Jean Jacques (1958). *Lieutenant in Algeria*. Hutchinson, London.

Swiggett, Howard (1955). *March or Die*. Museum Press, London.

Topic Magazine (27th June 1962). 'Interview with General Gardy'.

Warner, Denis Ashton (1956). *Out of the Gun*. Hutchinson, London.

Weygand, Jacques (1951). *Légionnaire*. Paris.

Williams, Philip (December 1961). 'The French Army'. *Encounter Magazine*.

Index

Index

Kunassec, Lgnre, 68
Kupras, Lgnre, 105

Lacheroy, General, 148
Lafayette Escadrille, 90
Lalaine, 137, 139
Laloy, Lgnre, 105
Lamy, Fort, 123
Langlais, Colonel, 138
Laos, 133
Lass, Lgnre, 105
Lautenbourg, 125
Le Clerc, Colonel, 123
Légion Étrangère (*see also* chapter headings for general subjects): Ranks, 30; Wine, 34; Foundation of, 50; in Spain (1835–8), 54–5; Constantine, Battle of, 55–6; Dress, 58–9; in Crimea, 60–1; '*Boudin*', 61; in Italy, 61–2; Kabylia (1857), 62–3; New Colour, 63; in Mexico, Ch. 8 (Camarone, 65–9; Santa Isabella, 69); Franco-Prussian War and Paris Commune, 71; North African colonization, 71ff.; Grenade cap-badge, 72; and Slave Trade, 76; Indo-China, 79–80; Madagascar, 80–1; World War I, Ch. 11; War with Abd El-Krim in Syria, 105ff.; World War II, Ch. 14; First mechanization, 121; Indo-China under Japan, 126ff.; *Groupement de la Légion*, 131; Dien Bien Phu, Ch. 16; Algerian War, 142ff.; Suez, 142; Mutiny in, Ch. 17; Organisation de l'Armée Secrète (OAS), 147, 148; Service du Moral et des Œuvres de la Légion Étrangére (SMOLE), 155
Lemeunier, Lieut-Col, 138
Leonard, Lgnre, 67
Loehndorff, Ernst, F., 27–30, 41–2, 45, 48
Londrés, Jacques, 27
Lopez, Lgnre, 105
Louis Philippe, King, 50
Lusiardi, Lgnre, 105
Lyautey, Marshal, 78, 102, 112, 152

McLean, Lgnre, 115
MacMahon, Marie Patrice, Marshal, 57, 58, 61, 62–3

Madagascar, 80–1
Magenta, 61–2
Magnin, Lgnre, 68
Magnus, Maurice, 96
Magrin-Vernerey, Colonel, 119, 120, 121
Maine, Cpl, 67, 68
Maire, Fernand, Captain, 93, 96ff., 105, 118
Manington, George, 27, 77
March or Die, 141
Marco, Lgnre, 91
Marcollo, 62
Marshall, J. Woodall, 85ff., 90
Martin, A. L., Cpl, 15–16
Martin, Frederic, Lgnre, 14–15, 75, 83
Martin, Jean, Lgnre, 154
Martinez, Major, 63
Massu, General, 144
Maudet, 2nd-Lieut, 65–7
Maurois, André, 21
Maximilian, Archduke, 64, 70
M'Chounech, 58
Mediouna, 102, 103
Meknes, 39–40, 97
Meliana, 56
Mercer, Charles, 96
Messaoud, 103
Met, Major, 78
Mexico, Ch. 8
Mexico City, 64
Michez, Lgnre, 105
Midelt, 105
Milan, Colonel, 65–6, 67
Minaert, Lgnre, 79
Mogador, 112
Mollenbeek, Lieut, 100
Montesquieu, Marquis de, 93
Morlae, Edward, 89–90
Morocco, 109
Moulay-Ishmael, 64
Moulinier, Captain, 69
Mouret, Colonel, 57
Moyet, Manuel, 94

Napoleon, Prince, 119
Narvik, 120
Navarin Farm, 91
Navarre, Henri, General, 135ff.
Négrier, General, 27, 71, 72ff., 79
New York Times, 26
Nielsen, Lgnre, 131–2

Index